The Ultimate Bridal Shower Idea Book

How to Have a Fun, Fabulous, and Memorable Party

Sharon Naylor

PRIMA PUBLISHING

Published in the United States by Three Rivers Press, an imprint of the Crown Publishing Group, a division of Random House, Inc.

THREE RIVERS PRESS and the Tugboat design are registered trademarks of Random House, Inc.

Originally published by Prima Publishing, Roseville, California, in 2003.

Library of Congress Cataloging-in-Publication Data
Naylor, Sharon.
    The ultimate bridal shower idea book : how to have a fun, fabulous, and memorable party / Sharon Naylor.—1st edition.
        p.   cm.
    Includes index.
    1. Showers (Parties). 2. Entertaining. I. Title
GV1472.7.S5   N39 2003
793.2—dc21   2002156407

ISBN 0-7615-6369-5

Printed in the United States of America

www.crownpublishing.com

10 9

First Edition

THREE RIVERS PRESS · NEW YORK

Contents

Part 3: Now This Is a Party!
Fifty Great Shower Themes

Acknowledgments

Many, many thanks to my acquisitions editor, Denise Sternad, from Prima Publishing, for giving me this wonderful project to spend my summer on, as well as to Michelle McCormack for her expert guidance on all of my books in the series. And big cheers and hugs to Jennifer Dougherty Hart for all she does to get the word out. My gratitude goes out to the entire editorial and marketing teams at Prima and Random House for their top-notch support and brilliant ideas.

Thank you, thank you, thank you, to my dearest of friends—Jill, Susan, Jen, Pam, Susan D., Loretta, Kristen, Julie, and Linda—who shower me with all the comfort, laughter, adventures, and pure acceptance I could ever hope for. I promise not to make you wear peach-colored ball gowns with high necklines at the wedding. How do you feel about sage-green strapless?

Introduction

So, what's the key to throwing a *great* bridal shower? As you're sitting down to start on the who, where, when, and what for this very important party, you're probably wondering how you can put together *the* shower of a lifetime, the shower of the bride's dreams. The bride is obviously very important to you, you love her very much, and you want to create a shower she'll not only enjoy, but remember forever with nothing but smiles and "now *that* was a great shower!" memories. And if you do it right, all the guests will feel the same way.

Nervous? If you are, fear not. Lots of women start this process under a mountain of pressure, sweating the details and hoping the party they plan turns out to be a huge success and not a boring, cheesy, yawn-fest that even the bride can't wait to be done with. (If you've ever been to one of the latter endless types, you know what I'm talking about!) Sure, it's an important task, but with your creativity, your pure desire to plan the shower of the bride's dreams, and the help of all of the ideas in this book, you're already well on your way to shower-planning success! Not too long from now, you'll have created from scratch one *fabulous* party, starting the bride off on her road to wedded bliss with not only a boatload of amazing presents, but the heart-warming assurance that she is adored by you and by everyone on the guest list as well. And *that's* the real goal here.

So what makes a great bridal shower? It's not just gourmet finger food, origami-folded napkins, raspberry-filled starfish-shaped chocolate favors in pink cellophane bags with the bride's initials stamped on them in gold print, kicky fluorescent martinis, or a fine merlot in crystal glasses. These are all beautiful accents and, indeed, some of the details that make an already-amazing shower pretty, stylish, and sophisticated. But they're not guarantees of success in and of themselves. What catapults the success level of a shower is that it's all about the bride (and the groom, too, if it's a co-ed shower). Personalize it. Choose elements and a theme that's really *her,* including all of the things and people she loves. She doesn't want or deserve a cookie-cutter shower, so go to great lengths to make sure this party is one-of-a-kind, just like her.

Another key factor is that the shower is *unique.* Think of every other bridal shower you've been to . . . think of the games, the menu, the cake decoration, the general way things usually go . . . and then see where you can make it original, irreverent, laugh-out-loud amusing, indulgent, and just plain ol' fun. This book is going to help you choose from thousands of fun ideas, which will make your job a lot easier.

It's Not Your Mother's Shower

By far, the smartest shower hosts these days know that showers have changed from the old days, just as weddings have. Today's showers aren't like your mother's, with every stereotypical game you've ever heard of and canapés and wine spritzers on the menu. After all, in decades past, showers were meant to provide the bride with all the things she'd need to set up her first home with her husband-to-be—those blenders, measuring spoons, cooking utensils, pillows, his and hers towel sets, and all the other must-haves for domestic bliss wrapped up in pretty white wrapping paper with iridescent bows.

These days, the bride is very likely to have her household set up already. She has her own blender, coffeemaker, and Egyptian cotton sheet sets. This is an era in which the bride has lived on her own for years before getting engaged, or where the couple has lived together for quite some time before planning to marry. These couples don't need the complete kitchen appliance collection or a bucket full of utensils; they're just as likely to register for kayaks and mountain bikes or a collection of fine wines *in addition* to those blenders and his and hers towel sets.

Yes, times have changed. Second-time brides rightfully enjoy their own bridal showers, the couple's kids plan some showers, and now the men might be joining in at a stylish co-ed shower. The party itself might be held at a winery, a museum, on a beachside deck, or in an estate home's garden rather than at home or in a restaurant. The theme might be wild and racy (as in the lingerie shower), glamorous (as in the come-as-your-favorite-diva party), upscale (the food and wine shower), or completely indulgent (the pampering spa party).

In short, the bridal shower of the twenty-first century is no cookie-cutter affair, no repeat of every bridal shower held for the past fifty years. The old rules are pretty much out the window, and you have a world of ideas and freedom of planning at your disposal, taking the pressure and bundled nerves away and setting you on your way to planning an unforgettable, meaningful celebration the bride will adore.

I'm Not Made of Money . . . How am I Supposed to Afford This?

Before you panic, I have to assure you that this is *not* going to be a full-time job and your whole life for the next six months. It's not a wedding you're planning here, it's just a fun party. Most of the bridal shower hosts I spoke to said they completed the planning in less than three months, devoting just a few hours each week to it, and they had the full support and assistance of the other bridal party members, the mothers, and even the brides themselves!

Planning a great shower is usually the result of a team effort, with several people sharing the work and expenses. You can plan a fabulous shower on a budget, with the right decisions making the shower *look* more expensive than it is. Add in the fact that creativity is free and a shower is more about meaning than price, and you don't have a lot to worry about. If you do have money on your mind, I've provided you with an entire chapter on budget ideas and sneaky little ways to make your favors, decor, menu, invitations, and even gifts look like you broke into your 401K and your mutual funds to pay for them, when in fact you haven't spent a lot at all.

As far as workload, I've also come to your rescue with a feature on sharing and delegating the work among your friendly helpers, so you have time for your own life. Planning a shower shouldn't be a headache or a burden and, with the help of this book, it certainly won't be. Making the plans and sifting through ideas, coming up with themes and building a party around all those great elements—that's a large part of the fun. Excited now? Great! Let's get started . . .

Other Books by Sharon Naylor

100 Reasons to Keep Him/100 Reasons to Dump Him

1001 Ways to Have a Dazzling Second Wedding

How to Have a Fabulous Wedding for $10,000 or Less

How to Plan an Elegant Wedding in 6 Months or Less

The Complete Outdoor Wedding Planner

The Mother-of-the-Bride Book

The New Honeymoon Planner

PART I

Planning Basics

Who's in Charge Here?

If you're reading this book, chances are *you're* in the lead position for planning the shower. In most cases, it's the maid or matron of honor (likely you) who takes on the role of main organizer and host, with the rest of the bridesmaids supporting in many ways as your partners. Someone has to be in charge, for efficiency's sake, and every good team needs a leader. The best leader knows, however, that it's a group effort, that everyone's opinion counts, and that the shower will come together much more wonderfully if you're a great "boss" to work with.

I've heard way too many stories of commanding and control-freak shower hosts who *tell* the rest of the bridesmaids what's going to be done, when, and for how much. It's *their* party, *they* know best, and everyone else had better listen to *them*. On the flip side of the control-freak shower host who runs the show like a boot camp is the emotionally detached host who can't (or won't) handle the responsibility and delegates every little task to the others. When I hear these complaints from bridesmaids—and even from brides—it makes me cringe in sympathy for their stressed-out attendants. (Not that *you're* going to be that way, of course!)

It's so easy to avoid these kinds of shower-wrecking and stress-inducing problems right from the start, by happily accepting your role as the Woman in Charge and then working with the other hosts to create a plan that's comfortable for all of you. Here, then, are the first steps to take:

Talk with the Bride

Though a shower is traditionally a complete surprise for the bride, check in with her to see what she truly wants. As you read earlier, today's bride might be older and might already have all of the household gadgets and supplies she needs. Talking to her beforehand is the only way you'll really be able to gauge what kind of shower she has in mind.

Find out if your idea to plan a lingerie-gifts–only shower is something she'd like. She may have already stocked up on enough thongs, camisoles, and push-up bras to outfit the entire Ford Modeling Agency.

Get an idea of the couple's vision. Perhaps her fiancé would love a co-ed wine-and-cheese party, rather than the traditional women-only luncheon. Or, you might not be aware that the bride's daughter wants to help plan the party as well. Remember, the main goal here is to create a shower the bride is going to love, so go right to the source.

Tell her you're starting on the plans and you want to get her input from the start: what she wants, what she doesn't want, any must-haves she'd like you to know about.

Assess whether or not planning the shower as a surprise to the bride would work well. Many shower hosts have successfully pulled off the traditional surprise party, but in some cases—such as if the bride travels a lot at the last minute for work, or if she's only going to be in town for one weekend before the wedding—you might have to reveal the shower date, just for convenience's sake.

Find out where she's registered—this is vital information for your guests!

Talk with the Bride's Mother

Although the bounds of tradition state that the mother of the bride does not host a bridal shower, some moms are throwing etiquette out the window and getting in on the action by solo-planning a fabulous party for their daughters. In some cases, this is welcome news to the bridal party, who may be strapped for cash and time and only too glad to hand over the power to the woman who wants it most.

Even if the bride's mother isn't stepping into the "head hostess" role for this shower, she can be a *great* asset in the planning process. She might be perfectly instrumental in a surprise shower, delivering the delightfully oblivious bride to the festivities. She's ideal for providing all the names and addresses of the shower guests, or even volunteering to take on a task or two (or five or six!)

◆

Mom is great for insider knowledge. She may be able to tell you if another of the bride's friends, relatives, or colleagues is planning an additional shower for the bride. You'll need to know this, as it's usually proper for each shower host to invite the bridal party members to her event as well. But don't worry, you don't have to bring a big gift to every shower you attend; a small individual gift is fine.

◆

Get the scoop from Mom on a certain gift item the bride and groom have been dreaming about, but couldn't register for at the department store.

◆

Don't forget the mother of the groom! She too might be willing to contribute some ideas, help with the budget or the making of favors, or provide additional guest names and addresses. Especially if she's been in the shadows to a degree during the planning of the wedding, while the mother of the bride enjoys the brighter spotlight, this might be an event where the groom's mom can let her talents and enthusiasm shine. (An added bonus: your invitation to include the groom's mother as a welcome shower-planning partner might go a long way in the bride's efforts at creating a great relationship with her future mother-in-law.)

Meet with the Other Hosts

Gather the other hosts together for an informal planning meeting. This initial meeting gets the process

started, sometimes introduces bridesmaids to one another for the first time, and allows each woman to
chime in with her ideas for the party. It's also at this
first meeting that you and all the hosts should feel free
to talk about your abilities to help plan—whether you're
short on time or cash, for instance.

♥

Plan this meeting with ease and budget in mind.
Rather than go out for a pricey dinner, why not lunch or
brunch? Or meet at a coffee shop or bookstore cafe
where you can relax in plush chairs or spread out your
notepads on a clear tabletop. Invite the ladies to your
place for coffee and dessert, or meet at a local park for
an afternoon picnic. This meeting doesn't have to be a
fancy one. Your planning partners might already be
strained under the cost of the bridesmaids' dresses,
shoes, accessories, or even hotel reservations at a location wedding. Keeping things cheaper right now is sure
to please the group.

♥

If the bridesmaids are scattered across the country or
the world, still in college and cramming for finals, or in
any way just not able to make a group get-together, then
it's time to go to the Internet. Computer-savvy shower
hosts can send out an initial group e-mail, followed by
update e-mails throughout the process to keep everyone
up to speed. E-mail is obviously a great and inexpensive
way to share information, ask questions, and get the
word out quickly on changes in plans. Considering that
many busy people can check their messages in a flash
using their cell phones or hand-held PDAs, this is a
smart choice for the organized planner.

♥

If you prefer a Real-Time conversation but your partners are scattered to the four corners of the earth, set up a private Internet chat room and schedule a time for you all to "meet" there for a planning session. The bonus of this is: your chats can be printed out for future reference, as proof that, yes, that particular bridesmaid did agree to shop for the favors.

❤

If one or more of the other hosts can't do the e-mail or chat room thing, for whatever reason, arrange conference phone calls from time to time.

❤

Allow each of your planning partners to use her planning expertise. This ensures that the jobs will be done well, by someone who has a knack for them. For instance, one might be enthusiastic about being the one to collect all the caterers' brochures while another might be willing to make the cake. You'll get major points by asking everyone what they *feel* like doing, rather than handing out assignment sheets.

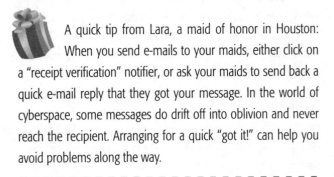

A quick tip from Lara, a maid of honor in Houston: When you send e-mails to your maids, either click on a "receipt verification" notifier, or ask your maids to send back a quick e-mail reply that they got your message. In the world of cyberspace, some messages do drift off into oblivion and never reach the recipient. Arranging for a quick "got it!" can help you avoid problems along the way.

Bring Up the B-Word

Discussing budget is a tricky thing, especially if your partners vary wildly in age, income bracket, and available funds. The wedding expenses themselves can be a strain on any person's budget, so don't be surprised if you hear a collective groan from your partners when you bring up the subject of money. You'll have to set a budget that works for all of you, so you need to start somewhere.

Not everyone is comfortable talking about their money situation (or lack of it) with others, especially if this is your first time meeting with them and you're a complete stranger. "So, how much money ya got?" just isn't the ideal icebreaker. In fact, it could even be quite the jawbreaker. You need to be a bit more tactful. The best way to broach the subject is to be direct about it, and throw in a touch of humor if you can. "So, ladies, as much as I hate to bring this up, we need to figure out how much money we'll all be able to contribute to the budget without selling our kidneys on e-Bay" would work. If you can get them to crack a smile, then you'll crack open the sensitive issue of money.

Let *them* figure out what they're willing to pay. "So, how do you want to do this? Should we put our heads together now and try to come up with a set budget? Or do you want to check in next week after we've done some solid research on what things cost, and then figure it out?"

For a personalized option, let everyone decide the dollar amount they can kick in, and have them write it on an index card along with their names and phone numbers or e-mail addresses. This privacy approach protects everyone's egos, and prevents any of the planners from feeling that they have to give the same amount as the bride's seven-figure-a-year CEO sister. For many groups of diverse shower planners with generous hearts, this option works well.

Handle the budget in a piecemeal fashion. By this, I mean you all agree to split the main expenses of the shower—say, the caterer's fee, including the cake—and then each co-host agrees to pay for whichever of the additional shower-planning tasks she agrees to take on. This is a great equalizer. The bridesmaid who's still in college and is living on less than $100 a week might be thrilled that she only has to kick in $20 for a few packs of shower invitations that she will write out herself, while the significantly more solvent cousin of the bride might be willing to buy all of the shower game prizes and the favors.

A great way to prevent back-and-forth bickering among hosts (hey, these kinds of battles happen all the time) is to state at the outset that each co-planner is free to spend whatever she likes on her chosen task. Regard-less of whether a co-host goes all out, or fools the eye into *thinking* she's gone all out with an excellent baker's job or a frequent-shopper discount at the craft store, you can keep the peace by practicing and encouraging discretion on the money subject. No one else needs to know what the bride's sister spent on the decorations, and no one else needs to know that you spent twice what the groom's sister spent, and so on. Don't get caught up in compare-contrast games when it comes to the planning, or you'll have a nightmare on your hands.

To get and stay organized, make your own worksheet with expense categories, and have each co-host sign her name next to the category on which she agrees to work. If two are sharing the responsibility for the entertainment, obviously both their names should be recorded there. As team leader, hang on to that signup sheet and make copies to distribute to the others so that everyone knows what everyone else is taking care of. This not only makes the planning easier for them, it also makes it easier for you when no one is calling you at 9 P.M. saying, "Hey, I saw a great deal on a wishing well for rent. Who's in charge of that?" With the photocopied list, they know whom to call. Organization is bliss.

Keep budget in mind if you're using the standard lump-sum arrangement, where everyone has agreed to split the final cost of the party. Look through the money-saving ideas in chapter 4 to see where you can shave a few bucks off the expenses, without cutting too deeply, and share these ideas with your co-hosts.

You can win the "Shower Hostess of the Year" award in the eyes of your fellow planners by letting everyone know that they can come to you if they're having trouble funding their chosen task. Show your flexibility and willingness to help, and the others are likely to become more generous with their time and money as well.

What about the bridesmaid or co-host who simply can't contribute financially? For instance, the bride's beloved younger sister may be completely tapped out after paying for the dress and the shoes. She simply cannot help pay for the shower, and she's really upset about it. While any bridesmaid always holds the option of not participating in a shower due to financial (or time) constraints, consider the concept that time is as valuable a commodity as money. Rather than writing a check, the bridesmaid who can't kick in $200 as her share of the shower expenses might be the one to do the errands, shopping, interviewing of caterers, or another of the many little time-consuming tasks to be handled. Let her choose a handful of tasks for herself, and then continue

Lisa from Davenport, Iowa, reports that one of her maids fell upon hard times financially and really dreaded calling her maid of honor to say she'd need help paying for the liquor, which she'd originally agreed to do on her own. Without any judgments, the maid of honor asked two of the more well-off maids if they'd be willing to send over an extra $20 each, and they were happy to do so. That cash-strapped maid then only had to pay for one-third of her original estimate, which was a welcome relief to her and a solution to the problem.

on with your original plans to let the others help out where they can as well.

Obviously, the more co-hosts you have, the more people you have to split the bill. So if the bride has chosen seven bridesmaids in her bridal party, everything can get just a little bit less expensive for everyone.

If it's a co-ed shower, that's twice the number of co-hosts. So don't be shy about calling the best man and having him and the boys pay for that liquor bill and half the group gift expense. The men might be new at attending co-ed showers, so it's your responsibility to welcome them to the financial side of hosting the party. In this instance, it's not just woman's work. The men get to open their wallets—and help with the planning—as well.

Share the Load

It might not be anywhere near the workload involved in planning a wedding, but pulling together all the elements and tiny tasks involved in a great shower takes a lot of effort. It's up to you just how many of these tasks you want to take on yourself.

Some hosts prefer to do most of the work, and farm out the little things to their co-hosts. For them, this is fun and they wouldn't want it any other way. If you're not the content little planner and would rather share the joys of making a hundred favor labels, spooning six different kinds of fondue dipping sauces into little white ramekins, and photocopying game playing cards, then it's time for you to delegate out the little jobs.

◆

Your planning team has already sifted through the major tasks, and decided who has the time and the budget to assume responsibility for each. Those are the money-oriented jobs and usually the first ones co-hosts think about when they consider the work that's going into creating this event. But the to-do list doesn't stop there. Next, there's an entire lineup of non-monetary tasks that someone has to raise a hand for. Before getting into these, make sure all of the major tasks have been assigned—someone's getting or making the cake and someone's getting or making the invitations, filling them out, and sending them. The task countdown on page 15 leads you through the major particulars that have to be covered.

The Little Stuff

Your to-do list is likely to be quite unique and detailed, especially if you choose from among the 50 themes listed here in this book. So you won't find "Pick up a jeweled medieval princess cone hat with flowing purple veil and matching magic wand" on the following list. I encourage you to create your own master task list either in writing or on your computer, leaving plenty of room at the bottom for the inevitable new and little jobs that will arise. Leave nothing to chance or memory. Write *everything* down, including who has agreed to bring in the tarot card reader and who's hiring the three impossibly chiseled male exotic dancers who will be pouring the wine for the ladies (and of course keeping their pants on—at least until the bride's mother leaves).

With your taskmaster list in hand, which you can quickly fill in at your first co-host meeting, you're already doing a terrific job of leading this shower to near-perfection. Be sure to pre-plan which of your co-hosts will be accountable for the following must-do's:

❤

Act as the surprise coordinator, pulling the strings and getting the timing just right so that the bride really does wind up being surprised when she stumbles into her bridal shower, and not her nephew's birthday party.

❤

Act as "introductions maven," standing at the front entrance, handing out glasses of champagne or punch, and introducing guests to one another.

❤

Wrap and label party favors.

❤

Wrap and label game prizes.

❤

Write out game cards, name tags, and other printed items you'll need for the events of the day.

❤

Create the seating chart, if applicable, and set out place cards for each guest.

❤

Wrap the bridal party's big group gift to the bride (and groom).

❤

Act as "card queen," the person who makes sure all the co-hosts have signed the card that goes with the big gift.

❤

Act as "RSVP captain," calling each of the guests who haven't responded by the date requested.

❤

Act as gift delivery person, bringing to the shower all the presents from guests who couldn't make it, but sent generous presents in their stead.

❤

Print out maps to the party location, or clear and specific written directions, complete with current landmarks. You'll get extra points if you make them fun: "Turn left at the house with the enormous turkey-shaped mailbox. Someone has too much time on their hands!" or "When you turn left onto Filden Terrace, you'll pass the home of the bride's first boyfriend. Laugh at his misfortune in letting her get away." These kinds of unusual notes make the ride memorable and let guests know that they're headed toward a most entertaining event.

❤

Act as game leader for each game you'll play as a group. Serve as registrar for which gift came from which guest, so the bride can send the correct thank-you's after the party. To make it easier, write the item description right on the giver's greeting card and place all the cards in a pretty basket.

❤

Serve as the recorder of the bride's comments while she's opening her gifts. (See page 140 for some creative and original twists on this particular game!)

❤

Make the fake bouquet from all of the bows and ribbons the bride has pulled off her presents.

❤

Pre-clean the party location.

❤

Set up the party location.

❤

Work on the cleanup crew.

❤

Participate in the return-the-rented-items group.

❤

Help the bride get her gifts safely back home after the party.

❤

Be the photographer and/or videographer for the event. Get those all-important candids and footage of special moments.

❤

Be the gopher. If any supplies are missing at the last minute, you'll be the person to run to the nearest store for replacement items. (Sanity-saver hint: Get two or three different people to sign up for this job; you might be dispatching them on more than a few runs for additional ice, daiquiri mix, or camera batteries.)

Serve as the "designated whatever woman," which means that whatever comes up during the course of the party, it's up to you to find a way to make it work, create a distraction, or in some other way save the day with your ingenuity and sense of humor.

2

What's the Bride's Style?

Have you ever been to a shower that was so standard and cookie-cutter that *anyone* could have been sitting up there in the guest-of-honor chair, surrounded by all the beautifully wrapped presents and smiling faces? The same old shower games, a standard buffet menu with somewhat-dry baked ziti and tossed salad, a sheet cake with "Showers of Happiness" written in swirly pink script on the top, bunches of helium balloons, guests checking their watches way too often, and someone standing in the corner aiming the videocamera at four hours of a nice-but-bland party scene?

In the complete absence of personal touches related to the bride (or to the bride and groom if it's a co-ed shower), the party you plan could come off just as hollow and unimpressive. The mark of a great shower is that it's all about the bride and groom. Since we're all about planning a truly great shower, let's focus on how to create the day according to what the bride would love, who she is, what makes her laugh, and what just might make her cry tears of joy (for a welcome change from those occasional tears of frustration during the wedding planning process!).

If, instead, your plans make a bride walk away from her bridal shower feeling guilty, selfish, and/or upset because she didn't enjoy herself, you've clearly failed at planning a successful event. Obviously, you shouldn't plan a Casino Night co-ed shower when the groom has been in Gamblers Anonymous for three years, or a steak barbecue for a bride who is a staunch vegetarian and animal rights activist. Tailor the day to the guest of honor's personality and tastes, and fill it with lots of personal touches that she'll never forget . . . in a good way.

Many recent brides have told me that it wasn't until their bridal showers that they started to get excited, forget about the wedding details, and enjoy preparing for a life together with their grooms. In many ways, it reminded them to relax and enjoy, have fun, and that their weddings would be special no matter what color roses or napkins they chose, just because people like them and all of their loved ones would be there.

What Kind of Party Is "Her"?

This is a basic question, and one you can answer by asking the bride. Does she prefer a luncheon? A brunch? An evening dessert and coffee party? Does she like the elegant, high-style afternoon tea type of event, or is she more the type to kick off her shoes for a backyard bash and spontaneous Frisbee game with the girls? Very often, this comes down to the bride's schedule (perhaps the only time she has free is a Sunday evening three weeks before the wedding). So go to the bride and ask for her input on what she would prefer and what works for her schedule.

Kerri, from Chicago, wrote to me after coming home from her bridal shower, an event that was clearly not "her." Kerri's two maids of honor, her college roommates, both exemplify the classic trendy, upscale city woman with the Prada handbag, the tiny terrier carried with her everywhere, and her personal trainer and manicurist on her auto-dial. The shower these two women planned was absolutely perfect—for them. It was high-style, glitzy, and extravagant, and the menu featured the sushi and sake they loved.

While the two women had been in shower-planning heaven, the bride and many of the guests were less than thrilled. Few favored the items on the menu (some joked—the bride included—about calling to have pizzas delivered!), most felt uncomfortably underdressed, and the bride wondered what in the world her friends were thinking planning a theme party that wasn't even close to who she was and what she liked. Worst of all, Kerri felt guilty and selfish that she was so upset about her friends' inability to plan a shower that suited her tastes.

If going to the bride strikes you as spoiling the surprise, then go to the groom or to the bride's mother for their best advice.

Take into consideration what the bride is going through at this time. Is she severely stressed-out with her combination of heavy workload or studies at school, all of the wedding plans, and a particularly fierce three-way battle between her and the wedding-party mothers? If the bride would rather jump off a bridge than see another formally set table or elaborate floral arrangement, your best bet is to plan a party that removes her from her current issues.

If the bride is stressed, plan something laid-back and relaxed, laugh-out-loud fun and informal, as far away from the topics that frazzle her as possible. (And no, you can't give those meddling mothers the wrong date and place for the shower as a further removal of stress!) If you're looking at your friend the bride and seeing someone who clearly needs a festive afternoon, then design your plans around the escape that's going to lift her spirits and restore her to the vibrant woman you know and love.

Think about the bride's personality. This is the most important consideration because the casual bride with a great sense of humor is going to enjoy a fun-based party way more than the princess-y bride who wears pearls religiously, crosses her legs at the ankles, and drinks her cappuccino with one pinkie up. The bride who can laugh at herself will enjoy those shower games where everyone tells a favorite story about the bride's past dating life. If your beloved bride *is* that princess-y, pinkie-up, finishing-school graduate, then plan the day according to her standards.

When brainstorming for ideas to make the shower reflect the bride's favorite things, gather a group of those who know her best (her sisters, bridesmaids, groom, work friends, and so forth) and chat it out. What are her pas-

sions? The most memorable events of her life? Her favorite vacations? Her all-time favorite moments in time?
Her heroes? Her favorite things? What is the bride best
known for? Her sense of humor, her cooking, or the fact
that she can build an extension on the side of a house
without ever looking at a how-to book? What are her hob-
bies? Her signature sayings? When you think about her,
what's the first thing you think about?

Do any themes jump out at you as just so *her*? For some
brides, all you have to do is think for one second, and
immediately your head is nodding and the theme comes
alive in bright colors and surround-sound. You know the
bride well, so you know her deepest wishes and favorite
things. Your sister who loves the French Quarter in New
Orleans would love a Mardi-Gras-themed shower, for instance. The bride who stopped in front of the Victoria's
Secret display window and sighed audibly, wishing that
she could afford gorgeous lingerie and marabou high
heels, but has to pay off her student loans before any dis-
cretionary spending is allowed, is a shoe-in (get it?) for a
lingerie-gift shower. (Chapters 12 and 13 cover themes,
so flip through those pages to get the ideas rolling.)

What's the bride's social style? Does she like the big
event with lots of planned activities, plenty of guests,
and the requisite mingling, or is she the type to enjoy a
quieter get-together with just her closest friends and
relatives, sitting by the fire with glasses of chardonnay
and nothing but enjoyable conversation on the schedule? Some people just aren't social butterflies, and
some don't like enforced group fun. Be sure before you
whip out that clipboard and announce "Let the games

begin!" that the bride is not going to cringe and try her best not to hyperventilate while the guests mob her and cocoon her in a wedding dress made out of toilet paper and safety pins.

When It's Not Just About the Bride

If you're planning a co-ed shower, your group effort may be focused on making the shower all about the couple, in a style that both the male and female guests will enjoy. Are they a martini and hors d'oeuvres type of couple, mingling among their guests in semi-formal attire? Can you see them at a long family-style dinner table in their home, dishing out plates of Grandma's lasagna, breaking homemade bread, letting the wine flow, and celebrating loudly in family tradition?

◆

How does this great couple like to celebrate the big moments in their lives, and how can you make the shower an event they'll enjoy to the fullest? Think about their shared passions.

◆

Is it formal or casual? Are they formal-dinner–party types, super-social nightclub types, or quiet-evening–at-home-with-friends types? When planning the basics of their shared shower, and even while going through the specifics in the upcoming chapters, be sure to think about their identity as a couple. How did they meet? At a sporting event? At work? How can you incorporate that history into their day? Are there any themes that work perfectly for them, such as a New England clam bake to commemorate the fact that he proposed to her at sunset on Cape Cod?

◆

Hold the shower at their old hangout, at the college town bar they frequented every Friday night and where they shared their first flirtation, first dance, and first exchange of phone numbers.

◆

What are their future goals? If they've just bought a fixer-upper home that's their heart's desire, perhaps that co-ed shower can actually be a new-home–themed shower with gift certificates to a home improvement supply store or garden decor items on their wish list, or even—as has completely overjoyed some couples—a working shower, where the willing guests come in overalls and old sneak-

- -

A shower host in San Francisco wrote in with her fabulous co-ed shower idea: the bride and groom were art lovers. They met at a gallery opening and have steadily built a small but valuable art collection. It's something they love to pursue together. Knowing this about the couple, calling it their "defining characteristic," the host held their co-ed shower in a gallery that she rented for three hours one evening, served hors d'oeuvres and champagne to the guests, and then surprised the couple by pulling down one of the most admired paintings from the display wall and handing it to them as their pre-purchased wedding gift from the bridal party. Now, that's planning a co-ed shower that's perfectly personalized and leaves an impression.

- -

ers and help paint the porch or create the garden. A big barbecue afterward celebrates a job well done.

◆

If the bride and groom are completely different people (since we all know that opposites often attract!), it might be tough to create a co-ed shower that's perfect for both of them. She may be happy in a little black dress and heels at a cocktail party in their honor, and he might be the type to prefer volleyball on the beach with a dab of zinc oxide on his nose. What's the solution when the couple is incredibly diverse? Split the party! That's right, it's a two-for-one in the most unique and personalized way. The first half of the party is that elegant wine and cheese cocktail party, followed by cake and the opening of the gifts, and then everyone puts on their swimsuits to head out to the pool or the beach for sand, surf, and sun . . . or even a late-night swim under the stars. Who says a shower has to have one style, one theme? Combining the best of both worlds is the perfect solution.

◆

Still stumped? Just sit the bride and groom down and ask them for their ideas, especially if the couple is one of that unfortunate percentage who has somehow lost creative control over the wedding while parents run amok with the plans. This is the bride and groom's opportunity to have the celebration *they* want.

Pleasing the Crowd

Earlier in this chapter, you read about the shower guests who wanted to order a pizza rather than pick from a tray of strange little menu selections they couldn't identify. That example serves as a big reminder that not only do you have to please the bride with the shower plans, you also need to keep your guests' preferences in mind. After all, the bride *will* notice if her older aunts look mortified at the saucy nature of the theme or the games, if her friends are bored out of their minds, or if no one is eating the food. It's a delicate balance, and while you can never please everybody, you can certainly incorporate a range of elements and tastes that will give you a greater chance of making sure everyone has a terrific time.

❤

Talk to the bride, the mother of the bride, the mother of the groom, or the most in-the-know bridesmaid about the general age range and description of the shower guests. If the party will be heavily populated by elderly aunts or school-age children, those are important factors in helping you make appropriate theme and game choices.

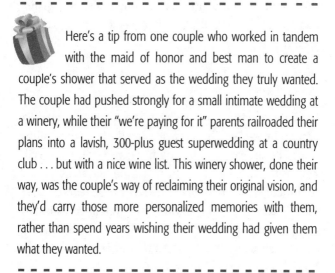

Here's a tip from one couple who worked in tandem with the maid of honor and best man to create a couple's shower that served as the wedding they truly wanted. The couple had pushed strongly for a small intimate wedding at a winery, while their "we're paying for it" parents railroaded their plans into a lavish, 300-plus guest superwedding at a country club . . . but with a nice wine list. This winery shower, done their way, was the couple's way of reclaiming their original vision, and they'd carry those more personalized memories with them, rather than spend years wishing their wedding had given them what they wanted.

Make sure you have smart choices on your menu and beverage list. At a shower I attended recently, the host made sure to include meat-free quiches and appetizers for her vegetarian guests, and also to stock sodas, juices, and ice at a bar separate from the liquor cabinet for the guests in recovery from alcoholism. That kind of thoughtfulness and care of the guests' needs and wishes makes the party all the better, the guests all the happier, and eliminates last-minute rushes to get food the guests can eat—or the need to call out for pizza.

Surprise! Or Is It?

The traditional bridal shower was usually a surprise party for the unsuspecting guest of honor but, as mentioned previously, in these hectic and jam-packed days, sometimes it's just more realistic to let the bride in on the plans and make everyone's life a little easier. It might not be as much fun, but sometimes the logistics and the bride's travel plans just make it necessary all around.

If you still want the shower to be a surprise, despite all the considerations, then enlist one or several surprise accomplices—whether it's another bridesmaid calling the bride in tears and having her come over to console her, or the mother of the bride taking her daughter out to lunch, only to deliver her to the celebration. In today's surprise bridal showers, the web of conspirators can get quite involved. Hosts can be devious when it comes to tricking the bride who has her eye out for potential surprises behind every door.

More than a few brides have written to tell me that their bosses played the key role in luring them into their parties, as in, "We have an emergency meeting with the account representatives tomorrow night. We're taking them to dinner to try to smooth out the issue." Sneaky!

The groom makes the perfect shower surprise facilitator. He knows her schedule, can easily create a decoy plan for an afternoon or evening meal, and is more aware than most what would really throw her off the trail. And the best kind of groom out there would love to play a part in helping his beautiful bride enjoy the surprise party she deserves.

If you're planning a couple's shower, don't discount the groom as the perfect surprise helper. Many hosts who have planned co-ed parties tell me it was actually better to have the groom in the know while the bride remained clueless. The groom becomes a valuable asset in the plans, since it's much tougher to surprise *two* guests of honor.

Brides with school-age children have reported to me that their kids were the lure. Children love surprises, and they love to be the center of attention. Okay, and they love to put one over on Mom.

The old "fake invitation" trick is a common ploy these days. With it being so easy to design a fake invitation on your

Though it may seem like something has been lost when the surprise element is gone from a shower, something good can also be gained. I spoke to several brides who knew about their bridal shower date, and they said they actually enjoyed knowing the big day was coming up. The anticipation of a fun party in their honor actually took the edge off the pre-wedding weeks and gave them something to look forward to: an afternoon of celebration and time spent with friends and family, rather than a day-planner filled line-for-line with endless tasks and errands.

Some brides also told me that they appreciated knowing which day the party was going to be because they wouldn't want to walk into a surprise shower wearing cutoffs, a T-shirt, and barely any makeup, with their hair in a ponytail.

"I loved my shower," says Brandy from Portland. "But I looked like hell when I showed up, and I look even worse in the photos and video! I stumbled into the surprise party after playing a round of mini-golf in 95-degree heat with my fiancé. ('Let's stop in for a drink at that restaurant and cool off!' he suggested.) And as nice as the shower was, I still hated being all sweaty and dressed down while everyone else looked so nicely put together. Shallow? Of course, but still . . . I wish it hadn't gone like that."

computer and print it on invitation card stock from an office supply store (or use an online invitation service like evite.com), you can easily print up an announcement for a supposed birthday party, anniversary celebration, or housewarming. Such an invitation showing up in the mail will get the bride to block off that party date on her schedule, without knowing the party is really for her! (Let the others in on the plan, though, since she'll catch on when no one else has been invited to Baby Joe's christening.)

Tell the bride the date, but hold the party the day before. One enterprising bridal party tricked the bride into thinking her shower would be on Sunday afternoon, when it was really taking place the night before. They had pre-planned for the bride to come out with them to dinner on Saturday, so that they could (wink, wink) "celebrate together first just as a small group." The unsuspecting bride dressed up for girls' night out and . . . Surprise!

Pick a date she'd never suspect. For many party-planning groups, this could mean a full four or five months before the wedding. At this point, the bride is not even thinking about when her shower is going to be. It's so far in advance, that surprise is almost certain. Plus, if she's a bride-to-be setting up a new home, she'll love getting all of those useful household presents sooner rather than later.

The guests need to keep the secret! While you can't guarantee that none of your guests will slip up and unintentionally give the surprise away, you can help your cause by making sure your guests are completely aware of the surprise factor, or the fact that the shower *won't* be a surprise so they needn't worry about slipping up. The best and most efficient way to let all of the guests know the surprise status of this particular shower is to write it on the invitations. A simple "Shhhh! It's a surprise!" is the universal sounding call that all your guests

- - - - - - - - - - - - - - - - -

One very bright 10-year-old from Georgia printed (on her home computer) a fake invitation for her Girl Scout troop's "Mother-Daughter Breakfast," to be held at a nearby hotel restaurant. Of course, Mom didn't suspect a thing, and she walked into her shower with the beaming Girl Scout in green as the master surprise planner. The bride was thrilled, and the daughter enjoyed her share of the attention and praise from all of the waiting shower guests.

- - - - - - - - - - - - - - - - - - - -

will understand. You can let guests off the hook from the pressure of keeping a secret by writing, "Don't worry! It's not a surprise party!" or "No secrets here! Dana's in on the fun!"

What's the Bride's Style of Gift?

When it comes to choosing the shower gift for the bride and groom, you have a great opportunity to give them the one thing they want the most. Very often, bridal parties and shower hosts pool their resources and choose the big-ticket item off the couple's registry as their group gift. It might be a complete set of Egyptian cotton bed linens, all their remaining china pattern items, a pair of mountain bikes, or home office equipment. Usually, it's that big box waiting in the corner to be opened last that gives the bride the biggest thrill— the gift that's perfect for her.

Talk with the rest of the shower hosts to see if they'd like to split the cost of a joint present, or if they'd like another arrangement. If some of the bridesmaids can't comfortably hand over $50 for their share of the crystal pattern, perhaps you can make the fund a "give what you can" pool. Each bridesmaid or host contributes an amount of her choosing, over a certain stated amount to keep it fair, and you as head host take that fund straight to the store to get the big gift.

◆

You may want to present the option of each person getting the bride an individual gift instead of the group getting a joint gift. It might be in everyone's best interest to give individual gifts or the big ticket items off the registry may have been snapped up by the bride's mother, other family members, or both sets of parents working the same joint-present selection.

◆

When looking at the registry, try to select the one item that you *know* the bride really wants, the most important item for her household, and perhaps the one gift that other guests are not likely to choose. With more and more couples registering for items beyond the usual blenders, toasters, and kitchen gadgets, the choices vary wildly. You might find yourself at a home-improvement store looking at porch swings, or at a sporting goods store looking for the waterskis the couple requested by make and model number. You know best what the couple *really* wants, so make this choice completely with their wish list in mind.

◆

When it's a co-ed shower, with all 10 or so bridal party members sharing the cost of the big gift for the couple, then you have greater options. You might get them the one really big-money gift, or a 12-piece set of some collection. Don't be hesitant to ask those groomsmen for their share of the present fund if they're understood as co-hosts for the party!

◆

Tie your gift in with the theme of the shower, if possible. For that lingerie shower, you might give the bride an extensive collection of silk robes, perfumes, scented bubble baths, and pillar candles with great candleholders. Throw in a basket of books on seduction, romantic gestures, or even "inspiring" erotic short stories or fiction. Include a how-to video on couple's massage techniques, and your big present becomes more than a collection of romantic items: it's an investment in the couple's relationship. What could be more appreciated than that?

◆

With co-ed showers gaining in popularity, the grooms are getting in on the personalized gift action as well. At some couples' parties, you might find the groom with a big smile on his face as he unwraps the power tool set he registered for. Next to him would be the equally smiling bride, who knows she'll soon have that bay window in their new home. Not all gifts have to be shared between the two; specific gifts for the groom are a big hit as well.

◆

Check chapter 9 for specific gift ideas, plus some unique presents given by real-life bridal parties to the guests of honor, and see if any of those stand out as the perfect gift for your bride and groom.

◆

If the bride and groom already have a fully stocked home and all the toys they could possibly want, if their registry has already been picked clean of realistic choices by generous relatives and friends at previous parties and additional showers, then what do you do? You could play sleuth and ask the groom if he has any ideas about what the bride would really love. Perhaps she hasn't registered for an item she doesn't think is an appropriate bridal gift, like a leather briefcase for work, or a membership to a better gym than the one she belongs to now. There's your answer, and there's going to be one very happy bride.

◆

A popular option now is making your big shower gift an enhancement to the honeymoon. When the bride and groom already have their house full of everything they need, then you might be able to prearrange such honeymoon treats as a sunset champagne cruise during their getaway or pre-pay a selection of spa treatments at their resort. Many cruises offer special deluxe arrangements for honeymooners, where you can choose from a half-dozen special packages including romantic candlelight dinners; flowers delivered to their suite; his and hers massages; scuba lessons; shore excursions in exciting and adventurous ports of call, such as whale-watching in Alaska, touring underground caverns in Bermuda, or snorkeling in the Cayman Islands. With a honeymoon-related gift, you've given the couple incredible and ultra-romantic experiences, those once-in-a-lifetime moments they'll keep with them forever.

3

Getting the Basics Together

I t's almost time to get to the fun part of the planning process, but first you'll have to sit down in front of that blank canvas and set down the basics: the who, when, and where for the party. Figuring out the guest list, finding the most convenient date and time for the bride and the guests, and setting out in search of a great and perhaps unique location for the shower might not be the most exciting aspects of the process, but they're certainly the most important.

Setting the Date

One of the most often asked questions when it comes to shower etiquette (along with "Who's invited?") is "When is it appropriate to hold the bridal shower? A week before the wedding? Two weeks?" The answer to that is: whatever works. There are no rules and no set time by which a bridal shower should take place. It all depends on what works best for the bride's (and groom's) schedule, as well as guests' availability.

The week or weekend before the wedding might be jam-packed for the bride and groom. With their hectic lives and busy schedules, some brides don't have a free weekend for weeks or months before the big day. That's why it's essential to check with the bride (or with the groom or the bride's mother) to find a date when she's available for a party in her honor. This might mean the shower takes place a month or even several months before the wedding.

Think about when the bride is likely to need her gifts. For instance, let's say the bride is graduating from college, buying a house with the groom, or relocating to a new city three months before the wedding. She's setting up their new home at that time, so why not throw the bridal shower close to that date? It's a great way to celebrate her big transition and also supply her with all of the appliances, home furnishings, and gadgets she'll need, right when she needs them.

Think about her special guests' schedules. If her sister or her mother isn't coming into town until a week before the wedding, see if you can hold off the shower plans so her most valued guests can make it. So many shower hosts don't think about this little detail ahead of time, and then they either have to scramble their plans or disappoint the bride when her best friend isn't there to share the day. This is a point to discuss with the bride herself, or with your inside contacts who might be able to save you from a scheduling snafu.

Take advantage of a special event that brings all the bride's special guests into the area. It might be a class reunion, homecoming, or your group's annual Labor Day weekend spent at the beach. Flip ahead in your calendar to see what's coming up.

Watch out for already-spoken-for dates in your social circle, such as another wedding or child's birthday. You don't want to tread on someone else's special day just because it's convenient for you, so be sure your proposed dates are all clear.

Who's on the Guest List?

If the bride and groom have invited 300-plus people to the wedding, does that mean you have to invite all 150 to 175 women on the list to the bridal shower? Nope. That's a larger guest list than at some weddings! While you certainly *could* choose to extend the invitation to every woman, most shower hosts give themselves a break by only inviting the bride's closest friends and family, the absolute have-to's among her loved ones. So how do you figure out who gets on the list and who doesn't? How do you handle that kind of pressure? Simple. You let the bride and possibly the mothers of the bride and groom in on the task.

◆

Ask the bride for her requested list of shower guests, and let *her* decide if she wants to approach her mother and future mother-in-law for their additional names. (This keeps you out of the fray, and lets the bride appropriately deal with pushy moms who seek to puff up the guest list to get the bride more presents!)

As the shower host and defender of your planning group's limited budget, you have every right to let the bride know the approximate number of guests you can invite. That lets her know you're operating within your financial abilities. A gracious bride will understand and work with you to provide an appropriate list of names. Many showers are limited to just an intimate group of guests: perhaps the bridesmaids, the bride's sisters and sisters-in-law, the groom's sisters and sisters-in-law, mothers and grandmothers, work friends, close friends, close cousins, nieces, and daughters. Looking at the guest list in "tiers," as in "We're inviting the bridesmaids, sisters, sisters-in-law, and the bride's closest circle of friends only," can help you reduce the head count.

Here's a big lifesaver in terms of the bride's future peace of mind and well-being. When drawing up the guest list, always be sure to include the most important women from the groom's side! That means his mother, sisters, nieces, best female friends, grandmother, godmother, or whomever. Too many shower hosts simply overlook that angle of the guest list, not thinking past going to the bride's mother for her input. The result can be slighted feelings on the other side of the wedding aisle and a wedge driven between the bride and her future in-laws before the wedding even happens! So ask specifically, of the bride herself or the groom's mother, which women from his side should make the cut.

When working on the guest list, ask around to see if anyone else is planning a shower for the bride. If her work friends or college roommates are planning their own celebrations, they don't have to be on your list as well.

◆

If you're a member of the bridal party, you'll undoubtedly be invited to all of the showers being held for your guest of honor. The other hosts know that, and you need not fall into the reciprocal invitation trap. To be clear, discuss with the other hosts your guest limit situation. They'll surely understand, as they are likely in the same position.

◆

People may be stretching the limits of wedding etiquette these days, but one rule still stands: Anyone invited to the shower must also be on the guest list for the wedding. No exceptions! It's just common decency and good sense. Breaking this rule is a shameless plug for presents from those who won't share in the big day. This breach of protocol could result in a nightmare for the bride, ending in broken relationships.

★   ◆

If the shower will be a couple's shower, that means that only a certain number of close guests can be invited, rather than a duplicate of the wedding guest list. Speak with the bride and groom for their couple's shower guest list, and mention your head count limit.

◆

The question always arises: What about faraway wedding guests you're almost certain won't be able to make it to the shower? Is sending an invitation to the shower when you know they can't come just a plea for gifts? No, it's not. It's a good-natured extension of the invitation, counting the bride's much-loved but faraway friends and family as important enough to be included in the shower day. It's not a plea for gifts, because it's the individual person's choice whether or not to send a gift when they can't come to the shower. They're not obligated, and they may be more likely to be upset if you've left them off the invitation list.

◆

Warning: Don't extend shower invitations to faraway guests thinking they won't come, so you don't need to figure them into your guest limit. You never know! Those 17 extra guests from clear across the country might get a great rate on airfare. Never extend an invitation you aren't willing to honor. Assumptions are a big no-no.

◆

Some shower hosts receive a lengthy guest list from the mothers who just assume that their list of additional guests will work into the plans. If the moms hand over a way-too-long guest list from their address books, you need to speak up in a diplomatic way. That means a polite phone call explaining the head count limit you've established and a request that they resubmit their top five or top ten choices. Clearly explain your situation and they'll most likely comply.

◆

You might find yourself in the same situation that's brought many a bride to tears: The mothers have already extended a verbal invitation to those 30 additional guests, and "What would people think?" if she called and uninvited them. Take a deep breath and decide for yourself if it's worth the fight. Talk calmly to the mothers and ask for their help with a fair solution. The best-mannered mothers might offer to kick in extra funds to cover their guests' expenses. Or you might wind up in a position where you'll have to find a way to stretch your budget or alter the shower plans to something different, less formal, and more affordable for a larger group than you expected. It's your move, it's your call. Every situation and every mother is individual, so proceed carefully.

My Place or Yours?

Most bridal showers are held at someone's home or at a private party room in a restaurant or hotel. The biggest advantage to the first option is that you really don't have to worry about availability the way you probably do with a restaurant or hotel. You don't have to hunt for a place that isn't fully booked, and you don't have to worry about hiring a hotel's caterer and baker as part of the package.

According to many wedding planners and wedding professionals I've spoken to, there's something very special about hosting a bridal shower in the bride's family home, way beyond the obvious convenience. It is cozy and warm, filled already with many important family memories, and brings a personalized ambience to the party. You're adding something sentimental to the home's history, and to the bride's future experiences in that house. An added bonus: She'll remember her shower every time she visits her mother's home, which makes the memory of the party last a very long time.

If home is where the party's at, you should do a little bit of advance scouting to see if the location is right. Is there enough room for all of the guests to gather and watch the gift opening, or to play the games as a group? At a shower I attended recently, the host's living room was so small that the women were packed together like sardines and sitting on the floor, which made for a very uncomfortable and *long* gift-opening period. A number of the guests couldn't fit into the room at all; some craned their necks to see from the hallway while others actually went outside rather than listen from the kitchen. You really need to make sure the home you choose has adequate space and seating for all.

The at-home shower presents a challenge when it comes to guests parking their cars. If the party is to be a surprise, the guests might have to park down the street, or use a willing neighbor's driveway (which is a possibility if the neighbor is a guest at the party). If you need your guests to park away from the house, then consider recruiting volunteer valets. Elderly or pregnant shower guests shouldn't be expected to park five blocks away and then walk, especially if it's hot or raining. At some parties, the co-hosts act as valets, and at some the groomsmen or the bride's siblings help out. Think in advance about the parking situation, and whether or not the home you have in mind is the best choice in that regard.

The at-home shower can add up to a bit of extra work in preparing the home and grounds for a big party scene. Here, then, are some of the must-do's for your setup process:

❑ Recruit a team of helpers from your co-host list to help the homeowner with pre-party cleaning.

It could be straightening up, polishing silverware, even cleaning the chandelier.

❑ If the party's outside, the homeowner (or
shower co-hosts) should be sure the lawn is
freshly cut, borders weeded, and yard cleared
of any pet droppings or debris from a recent
windy day.

❑ Clear the closet to make room for guests' coats.
It's just a more attractive and organized option
than dropping guests' jackets and bags on a bed.

❑ Clear the refrigerator of extra food items, take-
out boxes, leftovers, and other large items in
order to store the trays and menu items specifically for the party.

❑ Lock the doors to any private bedrooms or
other off-limit areas in the home.

❑ Add a strip of reflective tape or a spotlight to
any tricky steps in the home, such as that leading into a sunken living room or a surprisingly
high ledge leading to the outdoor deck. Bringing guests' attention to these hazards can prevent a trip, a fall, or even a lawsuit in the most
extreme cases. One source to check is your
local home maintenance stores, where you can
find inexpensive hazard tapes and even strips
of accent lighting encased in flexible plastic
tubing that's perfect for a run around the
underside of steps.

❑ Make plenty of extra ice, even storing extra bags
in a basement freezer or borrowed freezer unit.

❑ Stock the bathrooms with several rolls of extra
toilet paper, guest hand towels, air freshener
spray or a scented candle in a safe container, a

pretty fresh soap (perhaps in accordance with the shower theme), plus a tray of breath mints, pressed powder blotting sheets, and any additional toiletries your guests might need.

❏ Fill the home with a wonderful aroma. Perhaps decorate with fresh flowers; gardenias make the living room smell like paradise. A scented aromatherapy oil applied to light rings or scent diffusers can bring the smell of ocean air into the home. One party host told me that she baked a loaf of bread a half-hour before the party started, not only to serve with the clambake-themed menu, but also to fill the house with a cozy and homey scent.

❏ Watch the thermostat. If it's a warm day outside, get that air conditioner pumping for your guests' ultimate comfort and enjoyment. A packed house generates its own heat, as does the oven, so be sure to keep it cool inside. Same goes with the cooler months and your home's cozy warmth level.

❏ Have mercy on your guests' tolerance for pets. You may know that the owner's loveable Great Dane is an angel, but her mere size can make some guests ill at ease. Arrange for a play date for the dog, or ask if a non-guest can take the pet to the park for the day (which is a party for the animal as well). Run a lint roller over upholstered couches or chairs to lessen the risk of allergic reactions and help guests avoid errant hairs on their clothing.

❏ Set attractive, full-sized kitchen trash cans with lids at several locations inside and outside the home, so guests can toss their plates, cups, and utensils on their own. The benefit of putting out three or four trash cans lined with plastic garbage bags means you'll be less likely to find yourself hauling full trash bags to the garbage cans during the party.

❏ Set up a smokers' station outside if you have guests that smoke. This keeps the smokers away from the nonsmokers and prevents your puffing guests from grounding their cigarettes into the lawn. Get a pretty, colored-metal sand bucket, fill it with sand, and place it in an obvious location outside the front or back door, perhaps on a distant table or on a far edge of the deck railing. You might even stick a cute sign on the bucket, such as "Smoke Break" or "Get Your Butts Over Here." In case guests don't understand fully, stick a few disposed-of cigarettes in the sand for instruction.

❏ Assign a cleanup crew. After the party, the home needs to be completely straightened and cleaned, the trash taken out, and the family's belongings returned to their normal places.

❤

If you've decided to go with a private party room in a hotel or restaurant, you'll need to put in a little extra effort to find not only a great place, but one that's available on the party date and within your budget. This task could potentially take the most time of all of your shower-planning tasks, because you will have to go and visit the locations, ask questions of the manager, inquire about catering options, and find out which site is available and when.

A great timesaving way to round up location possibilities is to talk to friends and family in the area for their suggestions. Don't forget about your local corporate friends; perhaps their office holiday party was held at a great place, or a recent conference took them to a nearby hotel with a pretty poolside terrace that would be perfect. Use your connections and you might discover a fabulous site for the party.

If your guest list is on the large side and it looks like you'll have to get a banquet room for the party, do as the bride has done and check the newspaper's special wedding section, bridal Web sites with location-search options, or even regional bridal magazines. These great resources often list halls and hotel ballrooms, broken down by size and price, options and perks, special categories such as outdoor or country club settings, and editors' ratings for superior quality. Even better, you'll find complete contact information right there at your fingertips, with phone numbers to call and Web sites to visit.

Want to make a big impression and give the bride and her guests a shower experience they'll never forget? Go unique, with a choice of location that's as far as possible from the standard hotel banquet room with its round tables and crystal chandelier. The new trend in bridal showers these days is to take the party someplace fabulous, to an original and highly personalized location. Consider the following options for women-only or co-ed showers as appropriate and according to what stands out as perfect for your guest(s) of honor:

A winery's private tasting room

A restaurant with an ocean or mountain view, featuring a terrace or deck that allows both inside and outside access

A historical estate home, with access to its fabulously manicured gardens and private library with high-backed leather chairs and roaring fireplace (Check with the area's historical society or Chamber of Commerce for a listing of estate homes that rent their property for private events.)

A dinner cruise aboard an enclosed private yacht

A day spa's private party room (Check www.spafinder.com to find resort spas, day spas, and luxury health spas near you; private event rooms are a growing trend at spas across the country, so ask specifically for that option.)

A friend's beach house or vacation home

An art gallery with a private party room

A botanical garden or arboretum (Many have ballrooms or smaller private party rooms, as well as outdoor terraces and gazebos surrounded by incredible landscaping and fountains.)

An elegant cigar bar, again with the leather banquettes and fireplace

A sports bar, for the couple who holds a shared passion for their favorite team

A nearby state park or wooded clearing, for a Shakespearean garden party or informal picnic setting

A university alumni private club

A corporate clubroom or lounge exclusively available to members for rental

A private room during a restaurant's ultra-classy and ultra-delicious brunch hours (Bonus points: an extensive selection of breakfast and luncheon menu options, an endless lineup of desserts, free mimosas perhaps, and a surprisingly lower price-per-guest than at a traditional catering hall for lunch.)

A private party room at a theater (Many theaters and arts centers have not only private boxes for their patrons' up-close viewing of the performance, but also private rooms or salons for after-the-show entertaining. Check with the manager of your nearby theater to see if this is an option.)

A luxury box at a sporting event (It's not only professional stadiums that offer skyboxes and private VIP rooms; more and more regional and minor-league stadiums feature outstanding boxes.)

One of my favorites: Reserve an upscale hotel's presidential suite or penthouse suite for the shower if you have a small-to-medium-size guest list. The party takes place in a gorgeous, elegantly appointed suite with a fabulous view, and then—surprise!—the groom shows up with the bride's packed suitcase, since the room has been reserved for their use for the night, compliments of the shower hosts.

❤

You *must* check out the site and the individual party room in person to get a good feel for its potential as the perfect site for your guest list. Too many hosts make the mistake of booking a room sight unseen, or based on an image from a Web site. That's how problems happen. This job has to be done in person, either by you or by one of your willing volunteers.

You can narrow down the options by getting the names of the bride's favorite places. For instance, if you know she loves that great Italian restaurant right by her office, that's a place to consider strongly. If her family frequents a great eatery in their hometown—it's the first place she wants to go whenever she comes to town—then there's a place to start. The advantages of choosing one of the bride's hotspots are:

1. You don't have to worry about the bride not liking the place or the food

2. If she's a true regular and a friend of the owner's, you might be able to net a significant discount or some free extras for a party in her honor

3. The surprise factor might hold up better when the co-conspirator takes her someplace familiar for "a quick drink"

4. Again, you make the place part of the memory because every time she goes back to that restaurant, she'll think back to her shower.

When you're looking at hotel or restaurant party rooms, make sure you'll have plenty of privacy for your event. Some restaurant party areas are just sections of the establishment, not closed off by a door or a sliding partition. If that's the case, think about whether or not you want a roomful of strangers watching you playing the games or listening in on the toasts and private jokes you plan to share. Without an established boundary to your location, you'll all have to keep it down to a greater degree and perhaps not have the laugh-out-loud fun you might have had if hidden from general view.

Renting What You Need

Regardless of whether the shower will be held at a home, restaurant, or specialty location such as a winery, you might need to round up some important supplies.

Ideally, you'll be able to borrow the things you need from friends or other guests, but you might have trouble finding someone who has a bubble-making machine or a portable wishing well just hanging around in the basement. When you've exhausted your possibilities for the items you need to borrow (serving platters, champagne glasses, candle holders, and so on), it's time to look into renting those special extras and necessities.

Start off by drawing up a *complete* list of everything you need. Choose from the following usuals, and then add any items your theme calls for:

Tables
Chairs
Tablecloths
Napkins
Table skirts
Dishes
Silverware
Glassware
Champagne glasses
Coffee cups and saucers
Serving dishes
Serving silverware

Silver platters
Wine fountains
Punch bowls
Tea and coffee urns
High chairs and booster
    seats
Extra lights
Extra freezer or refrigerator
Air conditioner, fans, or
    heaters
Tents (for outdoor
    showers)

Search for the best rental agency around by going to www.ararental.org, an association that lists accredited and well-rated rental agencies.

Look before you rent. Always go to the shop to inspect the merchandise visually, checking to see that the items are relatively new, in good shape, and fit what you're looking for. You don't want a big, nasty surprise when you open the crate of rented champagne glasses and discover chips, stains, watermarks, and (eww!) caked-on food from a previous party.

Recruit a volunteer to return all rented items before the deadline! It will be a terrible surprise if the rental shop charges you for a full extra day's use of their items when the return team doesn't turn everything in by noon.

Showers on a Budget

If money is on your mind, and you're concerned that you just don't have the budget for a truly great bridal shower, *relax!* It can be done—and done well—for far less than the grand total your imagination has you cringing at now. With the ideas in this chapter, you'll surely discover great ways to stretch your budget and still plan a terrific party, without any of your guests clucking their tongues at way-too-obvious money-savers (well, except for maybe that one annoying aunt who finds fault with *everything,* but you can't please everybody!). All it takes is a little creativity, some great new resources, and a bit of legwork at the outset.

Invitations

Those little packs of shower invitations found at your local card store don't cost a whole lot, but you might pay $3 to $5 for a pack of eight invites and envelopes, which you then have to spend time writing out by hand. Compare that to the $5 you might spend for a pack of 24 sheets of party-theme computer stationery, decorated with bridal graphics, balloon borders, even Mardi Gras or seashore designs to coincide with your theme. Pop that ready-to-go paper into your home computer's printer, and in just a short time, all of your invitations are printed out and finished. Look for pre-designed stationery in a wide variety of styles at office supply or paper stores. See the Paper Products Resources (page 293) for contact information.

When looking at paper for your invitation needs, go with plain old printer or all-purpose paper (called 20 lb. paper) rather than the fancy vellums, handmade papers with flower petal fragments pressed into the pages, and other styles that might look great but really aren't worth the extra expense. An exception might be a soft gloss paper, found in office supply stores. This shiny, smooth paper provides a great look, and makes the most out of color print from a laser printer or copier. This kind of paper is typically used for business brochures and eye-catching handouts. You might pay slightly more, but many hosts tell me they loved the more polished final appearance of the invitation on soft gloss paper, and it turned into a bigger bargain when the shower guest list was a bit larger. I recently paid $18 for a pack of 200 sheets of soft gloss paper, and I made great use out of the extras by using the same pack to print out game sheets for the party.

Don't spend extra on those matching decorated envelopes you'll find in the store display stand next to the decor-printed stationery. You can use plain white or colored envelopes for far, far less.

Standard-size, lighter invitations save money by not needing more than one postage stamp each. If you choose heavier papers or an oversize invitation, you may need two stamps on each. Small change, yes, but it can add up.

Repeat after me: *I will not waste money and annoy every guest on my list by sprinkling shiny, wedding-bell shaped confetti into every invitation before sealing the envelope!*

If you're absolutely sure that everyone on your guest list has an e-mail account, then why not make the entire thing free and easy by sending your bridal shower invitations via one of the online party invitation sites? Check out www.evite.com and www.hallmark.com to browse their selection of on-screen invitation styles (some are interactive and very, very funny!), in addition to their extra features, such as a spot on your party's Web page for your guests to register their RSVPs, the number of guests coming, and any comments they might like to make. The site then tallies the head count day by day.

Menu

Comparison shop among caterers to see what they charge for trays of hors d'oeuvres, entrées, and desserts. If you invest a bit of time, you can certainly find a better deal for chicken marsala and mini-quiches with just a bit of hunting around. It's the party hosts who book the first caterer they find who waste the most money.

◆

Limit your menu. Instead of four entrées, choose two. Instead of six appetizers, choose three. With the right choice in menu items, choosing unique and delicious dishes instead of going for a big spread of the usuals, you can impress your guests' tastes for far less.

◆

Obviously, avoid the pricier dishes and go with the more moderately priced ones.

◆

When you're looking at caterers' trays, ask to see how big they are. Very often, you can feed 20 guests by buying the smaller servings of each menu item, getting smaller trays for almost half price, rather than getting way too much (and dealing with huge amounts of leftovers) by buying those expensive full trays. This works if you have several menu options, perhaps ordering four or five smaller trays and bolstering your buffet table with a homemade salad and other appetizer options.

◆

You'll certainly make your vegetarian friends happy, but you can also save a fortune if you select one meat dish and then a choice of pastas, salads, and fish for the others. Depending upon how they are prepared, non-meat entrées are usually priced lower. Investigate the options of those pastas and other dishes to find truly original and delicious choices.

◆

Love your meats and seafood, but can't shell out for filet mignon and king crab legs? Mix it up! Choose a pasta dish that incorporates meats or clams, crab, and lobster for a taste of the good life without the exorbitant price tag.

◆

Don't pay caterers' prices for those little extras that you can get much less expensively as a separate buy somewhere else. For example, go to your local bakery to get a few loaves of bread to accompany the meal and slice them yourself.

◆

Or skip the caterer completely and look at the various party trays that you can buy frozen or fresh at a warehouse store such as Costco, Sam's Club, or BJ's Wholesale—see Resources (page 299) for these companies' Web sites. At these giant shopping centers, you can find well-priced trays of finger sandwiches, seafood platters filled with shrimp, crab legs, and calamari, veggie dipping platters, frozen mini-quiches and other appetizers, sushi plates, and a world of additional menu choices for competitive prices. The only edge is that you'll have to do the heating and the cooking yourselves.

◆

Warehouse stores aren't the only ones stocking big party trays. Comparison shop at supermarkets, sandwich shops (for their six-foot subs!), ethnic specialty stores, and other eateries around town to see how they've priced their catering goodies. Many of the menu options at these eateries are fresh and homemade.

◆

Enlist all those friends and relatives who have offered to help with the cooking! Let your co-hosts, the parents and siblings of the bride and groom, grandparents, friends, and neighbors pitch in by asking them to make their famous lasagna or goat cheese salad, their crab and corn bisque, or a selection of desserts. The bride's loved ones are usually only too happy to help out, and having their specialties on the menu or buffet table is an extra-special, personalized part of the event.

◆

If a potluck party is the norm among your circle of friends or an accepted tradition in your region, then by all means make it a potluck dinner or lunch! This practice might raise eyebrows in some areas of the country, but if it's no breach of etiquette in your world then don't be afraid to plan the party as such.

◆

Would you rather have someone else cook for you? If you're more likely to hold the shower in a restaurant with a chef or caterer supplying the food, then look into less expensive times of day. A five-star brunch at a restaurant or hotel might cost you $12 to $25 a person, but you'd spend literally thousands if you tried to buy and prepare the enormous range of buffet items they're likely to feature in that official spread. From seafood serving bars to prime-rib slicing stations, and eight to ten steaming serving trays filled with everything from cream-cheese-stuffed toast to eggs Benedict, crispy bacon, and pancakes with warm blueberry syrup—not to mention the free mimosas, champagne, and Bloody Marys that many serve—these big brunches are a terrific buy and an impressive meal for all of your guests. I'd say it's the number-one way to get the most from your menu budget with style, class, and elegance.

◆

Love the brunch idea but can't picture the male half of the co-ed guest list comfortable about dressing up and listening to live piano music as they sip their champagne and snack on petit fours? Then look to a slightly less upscale buffet. For the more laid-back crowd, you can find a great evening buffet at a hotel or restaurant, and even at some of the nicer sports bars where the food ranges from traditional game-fare of chicken wings, ribs, and mini-pizzas to spicy pastas, teriyaki chicken and pineapple kebobs, fried shrimp, linguine with veggies and chicken, and great garden salads.

♦

For a mouthwatering way to save on your menu, plan a dessert and champagne shower where the only things on the menu are bubbly and sweets. With the right selection of cakes, pies, mousses, pastries, and fruit dishes, you can create a fabulous menu at a fraction of the usual shower budget. Check out the money-saving ideas for desserts later in this chapter.

A truly genius idea from Kelly in New Jersey: "We booked the co-ed bridal shower for a private side room at a sports bar here in town, and when we asked the manager about his catering prices, he told us they have a free buffet every Friday night to keep the happy hour crowd hanging around. If we booked our party for that night, the free buffet would be open to us as well! So we had no food budget and only paid the bar tab! The rest of the hosts loved me for finding it, and the guests had a blast at our party and then mingling with the fun bar crowd afterward."

Drinks

When planning your beverage menu, limit the types of drinks you'll offer. There's no need to stock a full bar with all top-shelf brand names and every kind of mixer under the sun, unless you're on an unlimited budget and you're hosting a drink-loving crowd. Three or four different types of drinks are fine: white and red wines, a specialty martini, gin and tonic, beer, and soft drinks are a nice range of choices.

Punches are a popular option for the budget-friendly party. Check out the many recipes on www.foodtv.com for a selection of pretty punches, and add a little decoration in the form of heart-shaped ice cubes made from the punch itself (so as not to water down the concoction), scoops of colorful sherbet, and even pieces of fruit.

For the wine-lovers bar, do a little research on the best inexpensive vintages out there. At www.winespectator.com, you'll find constantly updated lists of the best new choices in merlots, chardonnays, sirahs, and others under $15. A fine, well-priced wine is an asset to any party, and a cheap wine will make the party . . . well, cheap. So take it from the experts and make wise choices in wines.

Shop for your entire liquor supply at a wholesale liquor distributor, found in the Yellow Pages or online. These shops may not have the snazzy decor and the classical music playing in the background, but you'll save a fortune on cases of wine, liquors, beer, soft drinks, and even ice for the party.

The nonalcoholic bridal shower is becoming a popular option for earlier events, such as breakfasts, brunches, and tea parties. If your crowd would be fine with punch, teas, and exotic flavored coffees, then skip the liquor purchase entirely.

Coffee is a mainstay at most showers, and I advise you *not* to cut corners by buying the cheapest, largest tin of ground coffee in the supermarket. Guests are quite particular about the taste of coffee, so insist on a freshly ground variety of a good brand at the best price possible. This is, after all, the last taste you're giving your guests, and a bitter cup to swallow can undo all of your great menu choices throughout the event.

Desserts

Let's start with the traditional sheet cake. Iced in white, with pink frilly umbrellas on top, these cakes are the usual at many showers. Surprisingly, they can come at quite a price. If you'd like to go with the sheet cake, then tell the baker you're serving 10 fewer guests than you actually are. A smaller cake will feed your guests, and you'll save a bit of money by not buying the largest cake available.

When dealing with cakes, it's the labor that makes the price go up. So forget about the fancy cake with the intricate frosting designs, sugar-paste roses, and ivy trellises, the architectural masterpieces of layered cakes reserved for weddings and 50th anniversary parties. They're pretty, but they're likely to blow your budget. Go with a plain sheet cake instead, frosted with regular or buttercream frosting.

Save even more by buying a plain sheet cake right out of the baker's or supermarket's refrigerated case and piping the wording on yourself. For just pennies, you can buy pre-made sugar-paste roses and pop a few on top, or top the cake with fresh flowers recommended by a florist as safe, edible blooms.

Check with your baker about the prices for different cake fillings and frostings. It might not cost you extra to get a chocolate filling rather than a strawberry one, or to add a lemon-flavored filling in addition to the plain buttercream one.

Don't go crazy with the desserts. Unless you're hosting a dessert party (and we'll get to that in chapter 6), you really only need a cake and one or two dessert options to make a sweet-toothed impression. Shower hosts report that chocolate-covered cherries and strawberries were a big hit among their guests, as were cream-filled and fruit-covered tarts, and a tray of mini-pastries at $20 for a dozen and a half. If your menu has pleased your guests, they won't have room for too many desserts anyway.

One great idea for inexpensive dessert options is cupcakes. These little "cakelets" will never go out of style, and you can make them yourself in just a few hours. Decorate the smoothly frosted cupcakes with inexpensive candies (Hershey's Kisses, for instance), sprinkles, piped-on words, or the bride's and groom's initials for a personalized touch that hardly puts a dent in your budget. Arrange the cupcakes in tiers or on a platter, or set them on each table for a sweet centerpiece (saving you even more money!).

Making desserts is another way your eager-to-help guests can pitch in and contribute to the day. Just ask those who have offered their culinary assistance to bring along a batch of their famous triple-fudge brownies, hot apple cobbler, or puffy meringue cloud cookies. If any of these are the bride's and groom's all-time favorites, the true taste of home, then all the better!

Decorations

Decorations set the tone for a party, especially if you've selected a theme, but you don't have to spend a fortune for a great look. I've heard from shower hosts who spent a mound of money on a giant balloon archway that cost more than the menu! That may be nice for the photos, but it's quite the cash drop.

Comparison shop at party stores to see where you can get those bunches of helium balloons for less. Same goes for those fun piñatas, table centerpieces, wall boards, and other party decor. You might need to shop at a few different stores, but you can certainly find great bargains here and there.

◆

Look for sales at party stores. Depending on the upcoming or just-past holiday season, you're likely to find great clearance and storewide sales several times a year. Avoid shopping at the party stores right before the biggest party seasons of the year, however. With the approach of Halloween, winter holidays, and New Year's, many party supply stores raise their prices.

◆

Use store coupons. Spread the word among your other shower hosts, and one or more of you might find discount tickets in the newspaper or in any of the various neighborhood coupon packets that are mailed to households a few times a year.

◆

Decorate with what you have! If, for instance, your party's theme calls for Mexican fiesta decor, complete with sombrero and maracas, then see if you can't round up a well-traveled donor with a great supply of Mexican items to lend.

◆

I love this idea for free decorations for seasonal parties. The great outdoors offers you a world of beautiful, natural decoration items, all for the taking. Gather your other shower hosts for a "plucking party." Grab a few buckets or baskets and head out to your backyard, the beach, or even a nearby park to collect colorful autumn leaves, pinecones, seashells, evergreen or holly tree cuttings, even sea- and sun-worn lengths of driftwood.

These donations by Mother Nature can be used as decor and decor accents for an authentic in-season celebration.

◆

Head to a farmer's market or supermarket produce section to load up on lemons, limes, oranges, pineapple, kiwi, and star fruit to create colorful baskets or serving plates of fruit as your centerpieces.

◆

For beach- or tropical-themed parties, go to a dollar store or craft supplies center to find small round glass bowls and an inexpensive bag of colorful rocks to line the bottoms of them. Then head out to the pet store to pick up a few dozen inexpensive goldfish or brightly colored freshwater fish. Right before the party, center each of your beach-themed tables with these stocked fish bowls for a "lively" centerpiece. After the party, give the fish to willing friends and family who'd like a new pet.

◆

Decor may not be necessary if you're holding the party at a location that provides its own. If the party room you've chosen offers a great view of a city skyline, the ocean, or mountains, you can't beat that backdrop. Similarly, some restaurant party rooms are so well appointed with their own decor that you don't have to add anything but a few touches here and there.

◆

You don't need to spend $100 on floral centerpieces. Choose a small, low-set bunch of flowers, tightly clustered, and set in a glass bowl with water (see chapter 7 for more on these centerpieces). It's a simple and elegant look, and it doesn't obstruct your guests' views.

◆

Make your centerpieces work double duty, for savings. Perhaps you can cluster the party favor boxes there, or make a pillar candle and candleholder set at the center of each table the surprise party game prize.

◆

Another double-duty idea is to create pretty bread-baskets, complete with butters and spreads, for the centers of each table instead of having the breadbasket on the buffet table.

◆

Serving pitchers of Sangria or lemonade to your guests? Wine? Punches? Ice water? Center your table with gorgeous decanters and carafes of these drinks, with several pitchers or even small punch bowls on each table, eliminating the cost of separate centerpieces. For bigger savings, use the location's collection of decanters or borrow some from friends and family for your home-hosted party.

◆

If your decor wouldn't be complete without candles, go to your local craft store for a wide variety of colorful pillar and tea light candles at an enormous savings over the pricey ones displayed at home decor stores. To make them last longer, freeze them before using. Always set candles in safe containers or hurricane lamps.

◆

For that floral look to complete your romantic and elegant setting, you'll make a big money mistake if you blindly go to the florist you've always gone to. Comparison shop among different florists, discount nurseries, wholesale floral distributors, nearby family-owned farms, and any other potential floral resources. You might be surprised at the significantly lower prices you'll find when you venture off your usual path, especially at the floral wholesalers.

◆

Another great resource for small potted flowering plants that are great for both centerpieces and game prizes is the supermarket, believe it or not. I visited the floral departments of several supermarkets and found adorable potted plants for just $3 each, less with a supermarket's club card. Double-duty again, and big savings on a sweet floral accent to your tables.

◆

For those unique decor items that fit in with your theme, don't bother buying when you can rent. Check out your nearby rental agencies for their novelty items and see the huge difference in price for one day's use of a wishing well or jeweled king and queen thrones. Party stores also rent these one-time items, so comparison shop.

◆

As any event coordinator can tell you, lighting can make a big impact on the decor and ambiance of any party room. But rather than hire an expert lighting and special effects technician, you can create mood lighting by way of candles on tabletops, borrowed candelabras on buffet tables, dimmer switches on room lights, and a roaring fireplace in a home living room. For an elegant look for free, use borrowed strings of white holiday lights and line them generously along ceiling beams, around stairway banisters, on mantels, and in graceful arches of doorways. (Label each string of lights with the donor's name for easy return to the lender after the party.)

Entertainment

No need to hire a band or a DJ. Although some of the most upper-crust bridal showers do feature live entertainment, yours needn't be a mini-wedding complete with the starlight ensemble and a six-piece orchestra.

❤

If you'd like musical accompaniment to your party, simply pop a few appropriate CDs into a CD player and let the entertainment roll on in the background. If you use your own or borrowed music, your entertainment budget will be $0.

❤

Make (or ask a friend to make) several compilation CDs of the couple's favorite songs, or a range of music you think would make the perfect background sounds for your party. No need to go shopping for new CDs when you can custom-blend your own shower soundtrack.

❤

Certain themes call for certain kinds of music. If you'd like to have steel drum music playing during your beach party bash or New Orleans jazz bringing your Mardi-Gras party to a Big-Easy level of authenticity, check at a music store or party supply shop for specialty CDs with the theme of your choice. Or ask around among family and friends for themed music CDs. Your friends who have hosted many a theme party of their own might have that perfect Renaissance-era chamber music CD stashed in their garage-sale bin. Borrowing is always preferable to buying.

If you're holding the shower at a restaurant or hotel ballroom, a gallery, or other established location, ask if they can pipe in music through their sound system. Very often, such places have pre-programmed play lists in a range of musical styles, from classical to easy listening to party music.

The entertainment can be in the form of a fortune teller, belly dancer, massage therapist, or, yes, even those gorgeous male dancers who have been hired to serve the hors d'oeuvres on silver platters and flex their pecs while offering you another helping. When you're hiring these types of party professionals, your only budget strategy is to research the competition thoroughly, ask friends who they hired and if they can recommend anyone by name, and save a bundle by hiring these by-the-hour experts for the shortest time-package possible. For many, that might be three hours, so consider the price as you assess the need for live entertainment.

Prizes and Favors

Prizes and favors needn't be expensive to make an impact. In fact, it's the little things that mean the most to the bride, the groom, and their guests.

Skip the pricey favors sold at many wedding Web sites and go right to your local craft store to find silver frames, candles and candleholders, potpourri bowls, and more for just a few dollars each. Buying in bulk offers additional savings, and you can't beat the prices at some of the more inexpensive and well-stocked craft centers.

A truly useful favor is one the guest will keep around for a while. So the mini silver picture frame is ideal. You can insert a meaningful poem or quote you've printed up on your computer, or use a color copier to duplicate a favorite picture of the bride and groom.

Another of my favorite sources for favors and gifts is the bookstore. Go right to the small gift books section and find gorgeous collections of quotes or poetry, fun gift books, humor books, decks of inspirational and idea-collection card packs, bookmarks, and other long-lasting gifts and favors that inspire and amuse for just a small amount of money.

Plants are another popular choice for favors and prizes, as mentioned earlier. Plus, giving a living thing as a favor reflects a meaningful sentiment on the long life of the marriage.

Sweets as favors can also mean a *sweet* saving of money. When checking out the offerings in chocolates and candies, you have several options that can give you big returns for a small payout. Specialty chocolate stores can create custom chocolate lollipops or white chocolate roses, pretty boxes of mixed truffles or chocolate-dipped fruit, baggies filled with rum balls or sour tarts, Gummi bears, peanut butter cups—you name it. Dressed up nicely in a tulle pouch or a golden foil-wrapped box, the presentation adds even more oomph to your selections.

This one is my favorites. Go to an accessories shop and find the racks of bracelets. Silver, multicolored, beaded, gemstone-studded, faux pearl, woven leather—the style doesn't matter. These fun accessories make great favors for your guests, and they come at a price of $4 to $7 each. And who doesn't appreciate a fun piece of jewelry as a gift?

Here's one for the socially conscious. As we move away from the age when favors are a must and people *really* counted on getting an engraved brandy snifter for their time and trouble of showing up for the party, you can skip the gift item and instead print out pretty cards that announce a donation to an important charity (of your choosing) in each guest's name. You may have given $5 or $10 for each person. The dollar amount doesn't matter. It's the generous thought that counts. And for those who might scoff at the gesture, appease those judgments by attaching a chocolate to each card, or one of those symbol gift pins you find at the card stores for just a dollar or two each. A $.99 guardian angel pin attached to a charity donation announcement is a nice touch.

Game prizes don't have to be showpieces for someone's trophy case, especially considering that the guest has won the prize for guessing the amount of dollar bills in your purse. Instead, why not give out a toy? Gimmicky toys and fun little gadgets from Toys R Us might bring about a treasure trove of fluorescent Slinkies, Barbie sunglasses, Wonder Woman key chains, and other light-hearted prize items sure to put a smile on the winner's face. Best of all, these items are inexpensive.

Upcoming chapters cover more on favors and prizes, so if these low-budget ideas don't inspire you, read on.

Photography and Videography

Again, this isn't a wedding you're planning! No need to hire any pros at thousands of dollars a pop. Just use your own camera to take great candid shots, recruit several volunteers among your other hosts to switch off on picture-taking duties so that someone isn't saddled with playing photojournalist all day, and get those terrific moments captured for posterity.

Same goes for the videocamera. All you need is one, aimed well during the fun portions of the party and used to tape greetings from the guests.

If someone on your host list or guest list owns a digital camera, ask him or her to bring it along to capture some immediate images to download for the bride and groom.

If you're among those who own an instant camera, take that along too, with plenty of film cartridges to capture priceless moments and facial expressions. (Note: these photos can be used as a game if you attach each image to a piece of paper or scrapbook page and ask guests to provide captions underneath each picture. Double-duty again!)

All the Little Extras

Kids are great for contributing homemade items, such as signs and banners done on a roll of paper, the back of wrapping paper, or poster board found at office supply shops and craft stores. This way, you don't need to buy an official bridal shower sign, and the kids get to show off their handiwork.

There is no need to purchase game cards. Print up all those questionnaires, quizzes, and quote cards on your home computer using pretty papers or even brightly colored index cards that can be used in a laser printer. Include a simple graphic from your word processing program, and you've created for free what too many uninformed hosts waste big money on.

Go by the golden rule: Rather than buying whatever you need, borrow it, make it, or rent it.

The Top 10 Items Borrowed for Bridal Showers:

1. Tablecloths	6. Music CDs and videos
2. Serving platters	7. Candles and candleholders
3. Coffee urns	8. Cameras and videocameras
4. Punch bowls	9. Decorations
5. Tables and chairs	10. China and silverware sets

Invitations

The invitations you send set the stage for the shower ahead. With the invitation, you let the guests know not only the date, time, and place of the party, but also the theme to look forward to and even what to wear! Today's shower invitations have come a long way from those pre-printed ones you'd buy at a card shop and fill out by hand. There's a *lot* more to invitations now, a lot more creativity and a lot more fun, which you'll find out about here.

Just remember, the invitation is the first impression you'll make on the guests, their first look at your party-planning expertise and artistry. So don't settle for the ho-hum traditional when you can so easily do much better.

All the Vital Info

Before we get into designing great invitations, it's important to remember the substance that goes with the style. That means including all of the vital information that the guests will need to attend (and find!) the party.

In addition to the must-haves of date, time, and place, be sure to provide directions to the party. You might include a map, a sheet of written directions, or the Web address of the restaurant or location where clear directions are posted.

Use first and last names for the guest(s) of honor and the host(s) you list on the invitation. Some guests may know two or three Jennifers or Susans getting married this year, and some guests may be relatives of the groom who aren't immediately familiar with the bride's name. I spent a few hours trying to figure out who an upcoming bridal shower was for when I recognized neither the bride's nor host's first names on the card. It took a few sheepish phone calls before I learned that it was a shower for my father's client's grandson's fiancée. The last name of the host would have tipped me off more easily.

Forget the old etiquette rules and print on the invitation where the bride and groom are registered. Provide the Web site too, if possible. (Another reason why last names are so important is that guests need to locate registries by the bride's or groom's last names.)

Make RSVP information clear, especially the "'respond by" date. Include both a phone number and e-mail where guests can contact you.

Let guests know if the party will be outdoors, on a beach, on a boat, or at some location they need to know about to plan their wardrobe accordingly. For instance, high heels do *not* work well in a grassy yard, so allow the guests to make smart dress choices according to what the weather or grounds will be like.

◎

If bathing suits are required for your backyard bash, let your guests know to bring them along, in addition to sunblock and shades. Sometimes you have to spell it out.

◎

If the party is to be casual, state that! Fun or funky wording can let the guests know they can dress down or wear their favorite sports jersey for a theme shower. If you have directions such as these for the guests, this is the place to put them.

◎

If you'll be setting up a Wishing Well (a collection of little household items such as spices, toothpicks, and cotton balls), note this on the invitation. Some hosts simply write "Wishing Well" on the bottom corner of the card—that gets the point across—and others have written adorable mini-poems, such as this one:

> *It's the little things that make a home*
> *From toothpicks to hair gel.*
> *So as Claire and Steve set up their house,*
> *We'll help with a Wishing Well.*
> *If you'd like to bring some cotton balls,*
> *Some spices or herbal teas,*
> *These "little things" will mean a lot*
> *And be sure to please.*

◎

Be sure to convey the theme of the party. Guests might be thrilled at the idea of a Mardi Gras or casino night theme, and pretty soon everyone will be abuzz about your great shower idea!

Let's say you have a lot of information to convey, such as detailed directions, or more than two bridal registries for the guests of honor. You can do as other shower hosts have done and create a special Web page for the party. Guests can log on, check out fun pictures of the bride and groom, shots of the host group during the planning stages, details on the theme, and special directions for guests (such as requests to dress a certain way for a theme party), and simply click a link that brings them right to the couple's registry pages. Such a fun Web site is a great extension to the official invitation, helps guests to remain informed, and gives the bride a fun site to see when the shower is over.

Store-Bought Invitations

Sure, you can order professionally printed shower invitations on pretty, pearlized card stock if that reflects the theme and formality level of your shower. Check the pretty formal and informal styles of single-panel invitations at www.invitations4sale.com for a wide range of appropriate cards with daisy, seashell, playful, or intricate design borders that work well for showers.

Not into ordering professionally printed invitations (too expensive) but don't like the look of those fill-in-the-blank bridal shower invites at your local card store (too plain)? You can find much more stylish and unique fill-in party invitations through www.maxandlucy.com. Consider this the A-list of store-bought stationery sites.

◆

When ordering invitations, rather than making them, be doubly sure of your guest head count and the number of invitations you'll need. Ordering too many is just a waste of money.

◆

If your guest list is on the small side, making the invitations might be more financially savvy, as many professional invitation printers require a minimum order of 50 or more.

◆

Still interested in those pretty, pastel fill-in-the-info invitations from the card or gift store? If that's your style, or if the theme of the card works perfectly for your party, then go for it! Enlist a helper to fill out the vital information, since writing the extensive details 20, 30, or 40 times over can be a big time- and hand-cruncher.

Make Your Own Invitations

It can be a big savings of both time and money to make the shower invitations yourself. Pre-printed invitation packs might run you $4 to $8 for a pack of 12—even more if it's an intricate style or designer name—while a single pack of 24 decorated stationery sheets with decor-filled and theme-matching borders might cost only $4 to $5 total. Plus, using a computer to print out 40 invitations takes just a few minutes, while writing out the same 40 by hand could take hours. You can use your computer and printer to address all the envelopes too!

Choose whether you'd like to create classic, elegant invitations, or go fun and colorful with a theme decor, border, or accents.

Start off with paper or card stock, found at stationery or office supply stores—see the Resources (page 292) for store Web sites. If you aren't already familiar with the range of decor-printed stationery sheets and ready-to-print glossy card designs, you're in for a treat. Many themes can be accommodated with decor papers that already exist. Or get plain glossy white or pastel paper and use your computer's graphic design program and color printer to create true originals, complete with a great color picture of the guest of honor, or a well-chosen stock photo that works with your theme.

For the less computer-savvy, you can always use a color copier at the office or a nearby copy shop to run off great invitations. Just use a white or pastel-colored sheet of paper on which you've printed your invitation wording, tape the picture or graphics you'd like to include as borders or top or bottom accents, and use that as your template. It couldn't be easier and it's extremely inexpensive to create custom-color invitations this way.

Another idea for the less techno-inclined: Print your invitations on pretty colored paper or card stock and apply theme-perfect stickers to each one. Kids can help with the sticker task.

Make even the simplest homemade invitation look extra special by overlaying it with a folder or sheet of colored vellum, which is see-through, cloudy, or pearlized paper that transforms the look of plain card stock or paper.

❤

Unique and artistic handmade papers that include pressed flowers, flecks of metallic materials, marbled background, and unique watermarks are available at paper suppliers. These can be used for the invitations or as decorative layers or folders for the invitation.

❤

Simply lay a slip of color-coordinated tissue paper over the print inside your invitation. It serves no purpose other than a bright burst of extra decor, but it is an elegant touch reminiscent of a wedding invitation.

❤

Need to add an accent to a homemade invitation? Go to the craft shop and check out the wall of home scrapbooking accessory packets, where a world of pre-cut theme shapes and designs are waiting for you: pink starfish,

A great idea from Mindy in Pittsburgh: "The groom gave us one of his favorite photos of the bride to use on our invitations. It's a great shot of her standing under an umbrella—how perfect is that?—at a tailgate party. She's smiling and the sun is setting behind her. We couldn't have asked for a better shower invitation picture!"

smiling suns and moons, Mardi Gras masks, wedding bells, teddy bears, sunflowers, and more. No spending hours cutting shapes out of oaktag, and the mass-produced designs are far more detailed and uniform.

❤

Try your hand at 3-D designs. A recent bridal shower for a couple who was getting married on a cruise ship featured a 3-D pop-out cruise ship. The host who made it confessed that she cut the picture out of a coloring book, colored it in with bright and light blues, and copied it 30 times on her office copier. She then cut each one out and pasted it onto a simple three-fold piece of paper (to make an accordion "spring"), then glued her 3-D creation onto the shower invitation card for a standout accent.

❤

Want some depth to your invitations? Kelly from Lancaster, Pennsylvania, used pearlized card stock to showcase her invitation wording, and glued on dozens of tiny pearls for some extra-special texture. Not able to use a regular envelope, of course, she slid each invitation into a plain, padded CD-mailer found at her office supply store.

❤

Have some fun with your borders. Using plain scissors, you can create wavy edges to your invitations. With the new shapes of pinking shears available at craft and fabric stores, you can create medieval brick shapes, diamonds, and rounded "pearl" edges.

❤

Punch it out! Again, the craft store is the place to go for intricate and theme-shaped hole punches. Choose large or small varieties of stars, hearts, suns, moons, flowers, fish, Cupids, wine bottles, and so on. Punch out accent shapes all over your invitations. For added contrast to make those shaped holes come alive, lay a lighter-colored sheet of paper behind the invitation card.

❤

If you're a crafty type (or can recruit a crafty type to help you), create lovely effects with rubber stamps and colored inks, shiny embossing, or wax seals.

❤

Copy one of the most popular styles of wedding invitations and attach a ribbon bow to the top or bottom of the invitation. Punch two small holes horizontally in the invitation and tie a color-coordinated ribbon through them. It's a great and easy touch to make even the simplest and most elegant invitations stand out.

❤

Postcards are a fine idea *only* if you can fit all the vital information on them in print that's big enough for people to read. While postcards offer a lot in the way of creativity, ease, and budget saving, they're not quite as efficient as a full-printed paper or card.

❤

Make the postage stamp reflect the theme! The U.S. Postal Service features a variety of postage stamps, from flowers to beach scenes, famous authors to fire-fighters (see the Web site www.usps.gov).

❤

For a matching envelope, you can buy those with the same pre-printed design, usually found on the same display rack as the designed stationery.

Use plain white or pastel-colored envelopes. Not only are darker-colored envelopes a little more expensive, some post office scanning machines have a hard time reading the addresses you've written on them! So while a black envelope with silver writing might sound like a great idea, artistically, check with your local post office to see if their machines can read them. They might have to be hand-canceled, which might ruin the effect of your envelope design. The same goes for envelopes that are pre-printed with swirls, designs, graphics, and glitter. Think twice about decorating the outside of these envelopes, and perhaps leave the high-styling design to the invitation itself.

It's What's Inside That Matters

Just as with a wedding invitation, you might need to enclose some extras in your invitation packet. Consider the following, all produced expertly on your computer, using card stock, index cards, or specialty papers—see Resources (page 292) for specialty paper sites:

Maps are easily printed out from mapquest.com. Or you can write out the directions, including easy-to-spot landmarks, or have an artist friend design fun, graphic-filled maps.

Enclose a decorated or colored index card with your request for guests to write or print out their favorite recipe, best advice for a happy marriage, or favorite memories of the guest(s) of honor. Instruct them to enclose the card with their gift.

Include something fun for your theme shower. Reflect the shower's theme in the item you choose. For instance, you might tape a poker chip inside the invitation to a Casino Night shower, or even include a more sizeable item in an invitation box mailer, such as a fortune cookie for your Orient party.

Again, *please* don't include a sprinkling of confetti in each invitation. Sure, it's festive, but it's a pain to vacuum up.

The Rules for Sending Invitations

Send invitations out three to four weeks before the party to give guests plenty of time to respond. Send invitations out even earlier to guests who might have to travel a long distance to attend. Do the same for all guests if you're holding the shower during a holiday or three-day weekend. People make plans early, so give them plenty of notice.

Before sending out your invitations, double-check with the groom or the mother of the bride to see that their guest list hasn't changed! Sometimes, during the planning of the wedding, the couple and their families find that they need to trim down their guest list to meet their budget (or they find that they can invite more people with a change in their location or formality plans). Since it's extremely bad form to invite someone to the shower who isn't invited to the wedding, it's best to double-check to be sure your guest list is okay.

◆

All adults over age 16 get their own invitations. Sure, it's easier to send one to a mother and daughter who live in the same household, but it's just nicer and more respectful of the daughter to give them separate invitations.

◆

If the party will be co-ed, be sure to address the invitation to both partners by name (as in Sarah Jones and Michael Kelly). When you're inviting a single friend to a co-ed party and can allow that person to bring a guest, it works just like any other official invitation (as in Danielle Smith and Guest).

◆

Create an organized way to keep track of your RSVPs. It might be a spreadsheet designed on your computer or a handwritten list on a legal pad. Whatever your method, be sure you have a good system in order to get an accurate head count.

◆

If it's a week before the party and you still haven't received an acceptance or regrets from some guests, you can either send reminder e-mails or call those etiquette offenders. The more harried among us might simply have let the time get away, or the invitation might be lost in a to-do pile. Whatever the cause, it's up to you as the host to track down missing RSVPs.

PART 2

Planning a Non-Theme Party

Menu and Beverages

You could design the most glorious bridal shower with gorgeous floral centerpieces, an arch of lavender and white balloons, and Baccarat crystal champagne glasses sparkling at each setting, but if the menu and beverages aren't first-rate, your shower might be a flop. Guests say it's the quality of food and drink that can set a shower above and beyond the rest, since lukewarm freezer-burned food just doesn't cut it. You want your guests to enjoy every bite, rave about the food, and sip those mimosas with smiles on their faces.

Some Rules About the Food

Always plan on a variety of dishes to please all of your guests' tastes. That means adding some tried-and-true standards like tossed salads and pasta dishes to a buffet table that includes more adventurous exotic foods or ethnic dishes that need identification tags so guests know what they are.

It may be a budget-saver, but including fewer meat dishes in your lineup is also a welcome surprise for your vegetarian or vegan friends. A veggie quiche or lasagna is just what the selective diner ordered.

Make your lineup healthful to a certain extent. One shower host called in with her 20/20 hindsight recollections of the party she planned, saying that many of the guests didn't go near the Alfredo sauce dishes, the Swiss cheese and cream–smothered chicken breasts, or the dessert buffet because they were all in a Weight Watchers support group and dutifully counting food "points." They cleaned out the veggie platter and the bowl of tossed salad and picked from the shrimp cocktail, but those pricey catered platters stood almost untouched. If you must, go with one or two truly sinful dishes and keep the rest on the healthful side.

Don't go crazy with the food. Sure you want to impress the guests and dazzle the bride (as well as her mother and future mother-in-law), but it's overkill to provide too many menu choices. And it's quality, not quantity that counts. What's a good rule of thumb for realistic catering numbers? Provide:

3 to 5 appetizer choices

2 to 4 entrée choices

1 to 3 dessert choices

What do guests prefer? A buffet or a sit-down meal? It depends on the guests on your list, so the choice is yours to ponder. Most of the wedding parties I have spoken with said their guests loved being able to make their own food choices at a well-appointed buffet table.

Go with the bride's favorite foods. Add in a dish that brings back special memories, such as her grandmother's famous meatballs or the teriyaki shrimp kebobs she couldn't get enough of during that vacation she and the girls took to the islands last year. Personalizing the menu is always a great choice and makes the shower even more meaningful for the bride.

If you're cooking for the party, take the advice of professional chefs and use the best ingredients you can find.

- -

Some real-life experience from Adrienne, shower host from Georgia: "We planned a sit-down dinner for our 12 guests and laid the platters out on the table for passing. It sounded like a good idea, and we really prepared great Southern dishes. But it was tough for our seated guests to pick up and hand along the big platters, or pass their dishes around so the nearest person could spoon out some greens. Once the chaos started, we all decided it was just better to walk around the table with our plates and help ourselves buffet-style. It was very disorganized, and our guests had to laugh off the unexpected chaos."

- -

That means top-quality olive oils, sauces, real meats, imported cheeses, super-fresh produce, and authentic ethnic food brands. The recipes will come out all the better, even though you may have paid a little bit more.

Presentation Counts!

Even a box of frozen appetizers can look like a catered platter of expensive delicacies if you garnish it beautifully with twists of lemon, sprigs of rosemary, or a dusting of bright red paprika. Look through any gourmet cooking magazine, illustrated cookbook, or on the Food Network, and you'll see that in-the-know chefs don't just plop their creations on a plate and serve it to their guests. They add little accents and swirls of sauces for an artistic flair and a picture-perfect display.

◆

Buying frozen foods from a warehouse store to save a few bucks? These chilled goodies, when cooked and placed on your platter, can instantly look like a catered tray if you garnish them with items of color, taste, and even a little creativity. Try the following most popular garnishes for any dish (even catered trays that can use a dash of extra style):

> Place a layer of brightly colored lettuces or salad mix on the platter under appropriate food for a decorative bed.

> Put olives, red peppers, cherry tomatoes, or other finger foods on toothpicks and spear them into the tops of mini-sandwiches for a festive look and an extra bite of flavor.

> Group sprigs or bunches of fragrant herbs such as rosemary, chives, or parsley on or around the foods.

Lemon, lime, orange, or grapefruit sections can be thinly wedged, even twisted, for a bright citrus accent to foods and drinks.

Chop or slice exotic fruits such as pineapple, star fruit, kiwi, guava, papaya, and fresh coconut and set them on and around suitable dishes.

Add simple croutons or shaped crackers to a salad or soup or the top of a creamy dish for a little crunch.

Cut curls of cold butter or vegetables to add texture and design to a dish. Use a vegetable peeler or cheese-slicing wand to carve curls out of carrots, apples, or even slightly warmed dark or white chocolate bars.

If you practice a bit, you can become a sculptor extraordinaire, turning radishes, apples, peppers, strawberries, kiwis, and other standards into tiny rosettes, hearts, and other fitting shapes.

Use a cookie cutter to press out any number of theme-suitable shapes from breads, vegetable slices, and even meats, seafood, cheeses, and desserts. (Hint: check out your local home decor or craft store for a wide variety of cookie cutters in tiny to oversize shapes.)

Sprinkle sugar, spices, or cocoa powder over a dish. For even more design, first place a stencil or an intricate doily over the dish, sprinkle the powder over the doily, and remove the doily to reveal a decorative design.

Squirt out swirls of sauces, such as chocolate, berry, caramel, marinara, or dipping sauces, over or next to a prepared dish for a splash of taste in fine design.

◆

Dress up your ice cubes for an eye-catching, attention-to-detail touch. When you're filling up your ice cube trays, pop into each section a raspberry, blueberry, blackberry, slice of lemon or lime, section of strawberry, or sprig of mint.

◆

Find something fun to garnish drink glasses. A candy cane slipped into a red martini can make holiday drinks look extra festive, and you can't beat the tiny paper umbrella for your frozen tropical drinks. Other ideas: colored straws or larger slices of fruit such as pineapple, cantaloupe, apple, orange, kiwi, or star fruit, either floating or placed on the rim of the glass.

◆

Use edible flowers to sprinkle in salads, float in punch bowls, or to decorate an entrée platter. Warning: Not all flowers are edible—some are even deadly—so talk to a specialty produce expert or gourmet store be for purchasing edible blooms. Do *not* attempt to get these flowers from a florist shop. A great online source for edible flowers is www.virtualvegetable.com. A few colorful edible flowers to consider for your garnishing purposes are: pansies, rose petals, nasturtiums, violas, sage, calendula, daisies, lilacs, orange blossoms, and geraniums. Be sure to wash your choices thoroughly to get off any residual pesticides, dirt, or tiny critters calling the petal folds "home."

◆

For more instruction on creating great garnishes, such as sugared flowers and fruits, chocolate leaves, and masterfully carved veggies, check your library or book-store for the following books, as well as other specialty titles on the topic:

> *How to Garnish,* by master culinary expert and renowned food presentation guru Harvey Rosen (Note: books and kits available in English and Spanish)

> *Garnishing: A Feast For your Eyes,* by Francis Talyn Lynch

> *More Edible Art: 75 Fresh Ideas for Garnishing,* by David Paul Larousse.

What's on the Menu?

You'll find many specific menu ideas in each of the theme party sections later in this book, but since not all showers are theme-based, I thought I'd provide you with some ideas for standard bridal showers that focus on style and elegance rather than a single theme. You can pick and choose from these lists, or use them as springboards to come up with ideas of your own.

Appetizers

> Antipasto with meats, cheeses, and marinated peppers and onions

> Artichokes with dipping sauces

> Barbecued meat strips with dipping sauces

> Blintzes (cheese or cheese with berries)

> Brie en croute

> Caviar and cream cheese on crackers, endive, or celery

> Caviar-and-cheese filled crêpes

Cheese platter with a variety of domestic and
    imported cheeses

Crab claws with dipping sauce

Crudité platter

Cucumber sandwiches

Deviled eggs

Dim sum

Dips: spinach, goat cheese, herb

Fruit kebobs

Grilled vegetables

Guacamole with dipping chips

Marinated lobster meat

Melon balls

Mini-rolls (pizza, burrito, egg rolls)

Mini-sandwiches: ham, turkey, sloppy joe, reuben

Nacho platters with refried beans, jalapeños, salsa,
    and sour cream

Oysters Rockefeller

Pâtés: duck, chicken, veal

Phyllo squares stuffed with meat or seafood filling

Pierogies with dipping sauces

Quesadillas

Quiches (cheese, vegetable, meat)

Shrimp cocktail

Shrimp or scallops wrapped with bacon

Spring rolls

Stuffed clams

Stuffed endive

Stuffed mushrooms

Tortellini salad with fresh vegetables

Buffet Items

In addition to all appetizer items mentioned:

Beef dishes: marinated tenderloins or medallions, barbecued beef

Chicken dishes: marsala, parmigiana, champagne, lemon, lo mein

Chili: mild or five-alarm with cheeses and bread

Chinese specialties: lo mein, egg rolls, General Tsao's chicken, moo goo gai pan

Fondue: vegetable or meat with dipping sauces

Japanese specialties: gyoza with dipping sauce, sushi

Pasta: manicotti, ravioli, ziti, stuffed shells, lasagna

Salads: tossed, Caesar, antipasto

Seafood bar: clams casino, shrimp cocktail, fried calamari, crab claws

Soups: lobster bisque, crab and corn chowder, tomato

Vegetables: steamed veggies, stuffed artichokes, creamed spinach, eggplant parmigiana

Sit-Down Dinner

Any items mentioned in previous sections, plus:

Barbecued chicken and ribs

Flounder francaise

Mexican roundup: burritos, enchiladas, tacos with bean and rice side dishes

Pasta: fettucine Alfredo, linguine with clam sauce, lasagna

Prime rib au jus with horseradish sauce

Salmon steaks

Veal dishes: parmigiana, piccata, marsala

Brunch

Breads, rolls, bagels, and muffins

Brie en brioche

Crêpes filled with berries and fruits, with whipped
cream topping

Crispy meat sides: bacon, sausage, Canadian ham

Eggs: scrambled, soft boiled, sunny-side up

Eggs Benedict

French toast with warm maple syrup

Omelets with a variety of fillings from cheeses to
veggies to meats

Prime rib or baked ham, sliced to order

Quiches: cheese, vegetable, seafood, meat

Spreads for breads: cream cheese variations with
caviar, vegetable, chives

Stuffed French toast with cream cheese and apple
or berry filling

Dessert selections: fruit tarts, mousse cups,
Napoleons, éclairs, puddings, pastries

Desserts

Cake: you name the flavor of cake, filling, and
frosting

Cheesecakes

Chocolate-covered cookies

Chocolate-covered strawberries and other fruits

Chocolate fondue

Chocolate mousse in champagne glasses or tartlets

Crème brûlée

Cupcakes

Fruit salad or ambrosia

Ice cream drizzled with Grand Marnier

Ice creams, sorbets, gelatos

Lemon mousse

Pastries: Napoleons, éclairs, chocolate-dipped
éclairs, rum cake

Petit fours, iced in your choice of colors

Pies: apple, pear, pecan, rhubarb, pumpkin, whatever's in season

Truffles

White chocolate mousse

On the Bar and Around the Room
Place small serving bowls or glasses filled with the following snacks around the room and on the bar, on
patio tables, in side sitting rooms, and even by the exit
foyer for guests' quick grabs:

Baguette slices or bagel crisps with different flavored spreads: lobster, parmesan, dill, caviar
cream cheese, salmon, crab, vegetable, roasted
red pepper, guacamole, salsa

Chocolate-covered mints

Flavored chips

Grissini or bread straws

Party mix

Peanuts

Pretzels

Beverages
Wine and soft drinks are fine, but you can get a lot
more creative than that, and give your guests a nice
range of delicious drinks to choose from:

Bloody Marys (for brunch or luncheon)

Champagne

Coffee, including flavored and international styles

Daiquiris: the brighter the color the better

Espresso and cappuccino

Hot chocolate: make it mint-flavored or white, frothy with marshmallows

Margaritas: a wide variety

Martinis: sour apple, Cosmopolitan, Mounds, startini, Tiffany blue martini

Mimosas (champagne and orange juice)

Mixed drinks: gin and tonics, cranberry and vodkas, White Russians, bay breezes

Piña coladas

Punches

Soft Drinks

Teas: flavored, chai, green

Wine: Chablis, chardonnay, merlot, sirah

Plus after-dinner drinks: port, cognac, brandy, Chambord

❤

Research your wines well so that you choose several fabulous vintages for the party. A great source to find top-notch wines and after-dinner drinks is www.wine-spectator.com, where you can learn all about which kinds of wines go with which kinds of dishes and discover the newest, hottest labels with the best ratings.

❤

Like the idea of a Tiffany-colored blue martini? Check out how to make technicolor martinis and other brightly colored, creative, and potent drinks such as margaritas, daiquiris, and mixers of the moment at www.cocktail.com. You may just find a new favorite signature drink for you!

❤

A great idea for drinks at the shower? Name the drink after the bride. Of course, Tiffany already has her blue martini, but you can create "Mindy's Mai Tai" or "Sarah's Petit Sirah." What bride wouldn't love having a drink named after her? Spread the joy by naming the libations at a co-ed shower after both bride and groom, or give the groom his own drink. "My Best Bud's Bud" doesn't count!

Decor

Sometimes it's that first impression when the guests and then the bride walk into a bridal shower that sets the tone for the party's success. Imagine transforming a bland living room or a plain party room into a color-filled wonderland with flowers, candles, and theme decor that just screams "You are in for a great time here!" Jaws will drop at what you've done with the place, and the guests may try just a little harder in the competition for who gets to take home the centerpieces. Best of all, the bride will look around wide-eyed, impressed at the lengths you've gone to create an amazing bridal shower environment just for her!

Transforming the Room

Whether it's someone's home or a "nothing but tables and chairs" private room in a restaurant, you have before you a blank canvas on which to paint the decor for the shower.

Take a good look at the theme of the shower, or at the color scheme of a non-theme shower. That is the starting point, and the best way to figure out what you're going to do with the room.

Move all extraneous furniture out of the way, move tables to the side of the room for a buffet, and make sure you have plenty of comfy seating for the guests. It's the arrangement of the tables and chairs that forms the design of the room and your best indication of which items will accent each surface.

If you can, remove any existing wall hangings, pictures, and things that don't work with your vision. Ask the homeowner if oversize paintings can come down temporarily, and if you can move those family portraits for now.

◎

When "painting" your shower room decor, always go for color! Choose the color palette to coordinate, perhaps white with pink, lavender, or hunter green, in varying shades that unite the look and make your party space a lovely range of hues. Tablecloths might be a lighter version of the deeper purple flowers, napkins can match the tablecloths, and balloons can be a mix of the light and darker colors. Color makes a room come alive, so choose wisely!

◎

Tablecloths are actually a terrific way to "paint" your room with color or patterns. So look past the bland white and pastel colors to brights, big block patterns, florals, and fun theme designs.

What you put *on* the tablecloths also works to decorate your space. So choose color-coordinated plates and glasses for each place setting. Don't stop at those decor-printed paper cups at the party supply store; look also at those brightly colored plastic martini glasses with zigzag stems and two-tone hues, available at party supply and craft shops.

Add color to each glass or pitcher with a brightly hued stirring utensil as well.

Decide what your big accent piece is going to be. A balloon rainbow created out of hundreds of bound-together helium balloons creating an entry archway gives that proverbial "crossing the threshold" feeling. A decorated throne for the bride might be jewel-studded and surrounded by a beautiful array of potted flowers, with a spotlight on her as the center of the room. A big item reflecting the theme might hold its place in a corner.

Transform the room with light! Use dimmer switches to soften the lighting in the room. Change the direction of track lighting so spotlights focus on the buffet table, decor items, or the bride. Or use single spotlights to accent the gift table, the gloriously constructed cake, a special photograph hanging on the wall, or an arrangement of plants and potted trees in the corner.

Change the light bulbs in the room! Instead of glaring floodlights, use amber or pale-colored "mood" light bulbs to give the room a softer glow.

String lengths of little white holiday lights, called "fairy" or "twinkle" lights, around the room, perhaps on stair handrails, mantels, and doorways for festive decor. If you can find strings of colored fairy lights, all the better! Check craft stores before or after the winter holiday season to stock up on strings of blue, pink, purple, and red lights that are out there in plentiful supply. (An extra bonus and reminder from the budget section: Post-holiday sales are a great time to stock up on strings of party lights, so mark your calendar now if the timing is right before the shower arrives!)

Strings of lights come in more than just white or colored bulbs. Although these items are a bit pricey, your local party store is probably loaded year-round with fun theme light strings, such as glowing tropical fish, pineapples, moons and stars, high-heeled shoes, cartoon and Disney characters, even chiles or jalapeños for your Mexican fiesta party.

Consider stringing paper lanterns about the room, on an outside terrace, or in the ceiling space of a cathedral-style room. At www.whirledplanet.com, you'll find over 20 different shapes and colors of recycled-paper lanterns.

◎

If you're throwing a fall or cold-weather shower, arrange to have the fireplace in the room lit with a roaring fire. A dancing fire in the fireplace is the perfect accent.

◎

Candles transform a room like nothing else. So whatever your theme or level of decor, think about how you can include pillar candles of varying heights and groupings, votives encircling the cake, even candles in tall dramatic candelabras or full-standing, Gothic brass candleholders borrowed from a friend's ritzy apartment. Even the most well-appointed room seems warmer and more elegant when the space is filled with candlelight.

◎

Use colored candles. Visit any craft store or home decor store such as Pier 1 (www.pier1.com) or Illuminations (www.illuminations.com) and you'll find an immensely wide range of colors from bright yellow to deep crimson to deep sea navy blue, in addition to color mixes.

◎

Choose candles that are unique, perhaps those with actual stones, pinecones, gemstones, seashells, or other visual accents embedded in them for an extra touch.

◎

For outside decor, line your driveway, front walk, lawn, or stairway with lit luminarias, which are hole-punched bags filled with sand and votive or tea candles. Check your local party supply store for themed and color-coordinated specialty luminaria bags and use them according to smart fire safety rules.

Centerpieces

A grouping of candles at the center of each table is a popular and effective centerpiece that adds to the ambience of the room. Choose pillar candles of varying heights and place them on a platter to catch melted wax runoff. Again, use a unified color scheme or mix and match in coordinating hues, laying a few fresh flowers at the base of each.

◆

Arrange votive candles on a tray along with fresh flowers and flower petals or colored florist stones. You can elevate several of the votives on circular-cut pieces of cork or foam to give a bit more dimension to the arrangement. Look around to find unique votive candleholders. Gift shops, craft stores, home decor shops, specialty candle catalogs, and Web sites offer a world of colors and designs. Plus, it's safer to have votives in holders especially designed for them.

◆

Pretty, simple glass bowls filled with water, floating candles, and flower petals create a wonderful look. At Illuminations.com, you'll find a wide range of floating candle designs.

◆

If you'd like to use flowers, forget about those overgrown, expensive floral arrangements that cost over $100 a pop. Yes, they're lovely, but they're more appropriate for the wedding. Instead, choose smaller, tightly bunched groupings of brightly colored flowers, cut low and set in a small, simple glass bowl of water. Some ideal flowers for these low-cut centerpiece bunches are:

Allium (some varieties of allium look like colored snowballs)

Anemones

Calla lilies (in white for that truly elegant centerpiece, and in a range of shades from yellow to pink, burgundy, salmon, even pale green; ask your florist about colored callas to wow the bride and guests)

Camellias

Chrysanthemums

Daffodils

Dahlias (some varieties come in ball shapes with curled petals, perfect for a tightly clustered grouping)

Daisies

Gerbera daisies (My favorites! These brightly colored daisies in literally hundreds of color tones are a bit larger than standard daisies, and a grouping makes a big visual impact. Prepare to pay more, though, because Gerberas are more fragile than standard daisies.)

Irises (great if you're going with a deep purple or lavender color theme)

Lilacs

Lilies of the valley (normally a filler flower, and also a bit more expensive, but a grouping of these is dainty and adorable for a centerpiece)

Peonies (look for the type that's like a tightly clustered rose, available in a wide range of pastel colors and brights)

Ranunculus (another of my favorites and a popular centerpiece choice, these look a lot like peonies or overly packed roses and also come in a wide range of colors, including two-tone)

Roses (sometimes you can't beat a classic!)

Tulips

Zinnias

◆

If you'd prefer a tall floral centerpiece, go for longer cuts of the flowers above, especially those calla lilies if your shower is a bit formal. Add in volume-givers such as long grasses, branches of cherry blossoms, or dogwood branches.

◆

Pretty bud vases with one or two fresh blooms at each table setting make for lovely table decor, and those vases become the guests' take-home favors. Center the table with a pillar candle, and you're all set with a deceptively inexpensive centerpieces.

◆

Tie your floral centerpiece into each place setting by laying a matching floral bloom across each plate or slipped into a ring-held napkin.

◆

For a party around the winter holidays, use evergreen branches and holly to make red roses stand out. You might be able to get the branches and holly right from the trees of a friend or neighbor and bring them freshly cut to the shower.

◆

Don't worry about finding a dozen crystal vases to hold your floral centerpieces. While you can find inexpensive small glass bowls to hold cut flower bunches, another option is using a bag. Place a florist's "frog" or block of foam in the bottom of a white or colored paper bag or one of those gorgeous decorated gift bags from the card store, and arrange your cut or potted flowers and fillers in those. You can also use a decorated gift bag designed for wine bottles and available at wine stores.

◆

You can arrange your centerpiece in a Lucite gift box, found in party supply shops or catalogs. These plastic boxes come in a range of colors and sizes, and might be the perfect holders for your centerpiece items.

◆

Here's a twist on the floating candle idea: Set several tall pillar candles in the center of the table. Around that grouping, set a number of classic or unique martini glasses. Fill the glasses halfway with water and place in each a white gardenia. The look is amazing, and the scent of the fresh gardenias will fill the room.

◆

In chapter 4, you read about using your finds from the farmer's market as centerpieces. Very often, it's these natural items, even green apples, bright orange pumpkins, and uniquely shaped gourds that make the best, homey centerpieces.

◆

Choose an item from your theme, such as a child-size sombrero for a Mexican theme, a bucket of sand and shells for a beach theme, a sports helmet for a pro-league theme, even a child's graciously lent supply of toys for a more playful party. These might be Barbie in her Camaro, or the Little Mermaid doll surrounded by shells and seahorses bought at a craft store.

◆

For a beach wedding, use a fishbowl with live, swimming, brightly colored fish at the center of each table.

◆

For an elegant, co-ed cigar and brandy party, you can place collections of cigars in great crystal glasses or bowls.

◆

In chapter 4, you read about setting pictures and portraits of the bride and groom at each table. Dress up those beautiful silver frames with a circle of votive candles or sprigs of lilies of the valley, heather, or baby's breath.

◆

Place special photo albums at the center of each table. Mini photo albums won't cost you a lot, and you can fill them with great shots of the family, the bride with her friends, the groom and his friends, and moments of the couple's long courtship.

◆

A good way to make even the most modest centerpiece look great is to set it on a mirror or silver platter. The mirror or silver extends the color of the centerpiece outward and reflects candlelight. This trick produces an elegant look and makes a big visual impact.

◆

Another way to add some extra oomph to any centerpiece is to scatter colorful flower petals around it. You might use rose petals in various coordinated colors, or check out the different shapes and curls of other flower petals. On darker tablecloths, you can't beat the look of white flower petals mixed with petals in a lighter shade of the tablecloth color.

◆

Scatter leaves on the table. Some flowers and potted plants produce gorgeous leaves in various colors, shapes, and designs, so after you've cut the flower heads for your centerpieces, strip off the leaves to use for scattering.

◆

Use sections of fern or Queen Anne's lace as table decor. Traditionally used as filler for bouquets and centerpieces, these earthy greens make wonderful table accents, and they're among the least expensive choices in the florist's shop. Just one or two bunches for a few dollars can embellish the whole room.

◆

Sprinkle the table with confetti—metallic, shiny, textured, tissue paper, or even thin wood confetti. Some designs are larger for easier cleanup and shape identification. Some of the most popular confetti shapes are:

Balloons

Bells

Cherubs

Flower petals

Flowers

Large or small hearts

Large or small hearts with the centers hollowed out

Lips

Moons

Stars

Umbrellas

◆

An interesting new table decor idea blowing onto the scene right now is feathers. Pretty colored sections of marabou feathers—*not* those fantasy dress-up boas!—placed on each table at the bottom of a floral bunch lends a dreamy look to your tables.

Fabrics

Ask any interior decorator and she or he will tell you that fabrics can transform a party room from lovely to fabulous. We've already touched on using the color of the tablecloths to create a color palette for the room; read on for additional fabric accents.

♥

Research rental companies (www.ararental.org) to find the ones with the largest selection of linen colors. Some companies just offer the usual whites, greens, and primary colors, plus a few pastels. Other companies stock a wider range of colors.

♥

Don't just stop at one tablecloth per table. You can add extra color and dimension by laying a second, smaller tablecloth, in a lighter hue of the same color, at an angle over the first tablecloth. Each table then shows both colors, adding extra visual impact.

♥

Another fabric overlay to your colored tablecloth might be a swath of delicate lace, if that works with the style, formality, and theme of your shower.

❤

Choose napkins that either match the tablecloth exactly or are in a lighter hue of the same color family. Such eye-catching accents can greatly enhance the appearance of each table.

❤

Having the shower at a home? Use fabrics as touches around the room. For instance, remove those animal-print throw pillows from that beige couch and toss on a few pillows that match the color theme for your party. Inexpensive throw pillows can be found at home decor stores, and you only need one or two to tie the sitting area into the rest of the room. Or lay a color-coordinated throw blanket over the back or arm of that beige couch.

❤

Use fabric to cover the backs of borrowed folding chairs. If you've borrowed chairs from your friends, but they all have different backs and just don't look coordinated, you can rent chair back covers to slip over each one.

❤

A colorful or ethnic-themed strip of fabric can serve as a table runner on your buffet, cake, or gift table for a bit of extra flair and a personalized touch.

❤

Window treatments present gorgeous possibilities for shower decor. Ask the homeowner if you can play around with the draping of her curtains. Practice gathering and swathing the fabric, twisting and lifting, to make that lace curtain a gracefully flowing fabric sculpture.

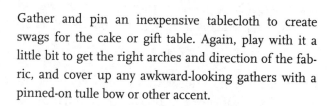

Gather and pin an inexpensive tablecloth to create swags for the cake or gift table. Again, play with it a little bit to get the right arches and direction of the fabric, and cover up any awkward-looking gathers with a pinned-on tulle bow or other accent.

Tulle is a catchall fabric for anything bridal. You can cut small sections and create bows to attach to the back of each chair, or you can cut a longer length and scrunch it up as the perfect surrounding to the cake. Drape longer lengths of tulle over curtain rods or over an inexpensive pressure-spring curtain rod installed in a doorway to create an ethereal entry.

Like the look of tulle? Check local fabric and craft stores for tulle in different colors. You might find just the right

Here's a tip from Dana in Connecticut: "We wanted the living room at the bride's mom's house to blend in with our color scheme, but she had this loud, patterned blue couch that clashed with our sage-green decor. So one of the bridesmaids volunteered to take the sage-green slipcover off her own couch, clean it, and put it on the mother's couch. She brought her sage and beige throw pillows as well, and that one little touch made the entire room look so much more 'together' with very little effort."

shade of blue, lavender, red, or pink to create even more fabric swags, bows, entryway curtains, even the curtain for staged appearances or party games you have in mind.

❤

Use a length of thick ribbon with a single flower bloom attached as a napkin ring. Ribbons come in all colors and textures. Rich velvet lends an elegant touch to a winter wedding.

In Print

A sign or banner reading "Showers of Happiness" strung across the far end of the room is always a nice touch, and it becomes a keepsake for the bride if you have all of the guests write a personal message on it before you put it up.

◉

Put signs and posters around the room—set on mantels or hung on the walls—that tie in with your theme. For instance, put up posters of exotic countries or cities for an international-themed party. A terrific source for theme or decor posters is www.allposters.com, where you'll find everything from garden to beach to big city designs at darn good prices. A great source for travel posters is your local travel agent's office. Since they change their displays often, they might have a stash of African safari or Hawaii posters in their back room.

◉

Another kind of printed decor is a blown-up photo of the bride. While some bridal parties have used her driver's license photo, you might choose a more fun and flattering shot of her, attached to thick poster board for a sturdy stand-up. Have the guests write messages of love and greetings around the outside of the picture for a heartfelt memento.

Other posters to display: blown-up pictures of the bride with her girlfriends, with her sisters, or with her daughter.

Place-card holders are now available in an enormous variety of styles, from pewter chairs to animal shapes, floral designs to festive sprays of colored cellophane. Check out www.beau-coup.com for their selection of elegant place-card holders, including lovely glass holders that contain a votive candle or a mini–bud vase.

Place cards can range from the usual handwritten name on a folded white piece of paper, or you can have a little fun with it. Check your office supply store for bright paper stock, textured paper, and even thicker card stock. For a great font and uniform writing, use your computer to print the place cards.

Attach a piece of candy, such as a wrapped Godiva chocolate or Hershey's Kiss, to each place card for a decoration and an extra sweet little something.

Attach a single tiny flower to each place card as decoration.

For beach or summer-themed showers, glue a tiny seashell, starfish, seahorse, or mini–drink umbrella to each place card.

A simple sticker or grouping of teeny stickers can tie a place card into an unusual theme. Go to your local crafts store and choose from flowers, wine bottles, cartoon characters, animals, stars and planets, and other graphics for a cute and inexpensive touch.

For a little extra fun with place cards and a great tie-in to a theme, be creative with the writing of guests' names. At a "Paris in Springtime" shower, the host wrote the French version of each guest's first name. At a really fun co-ed shower with a mobster theme, the hosts gave each guest a fictional Mob name. The bride's father, Benjamin Stone, became Bennie "The Chin" Stone. Have some fun with this, because you can really get your crowd laughing.

In place of printed place cards, use frosted sugar cookies with the names and table numbers written in icing. Bakers can work magic with cookie shapes and frosting colors, so choose a fun theme-oriented design.

Combine the place cards with the favors. For instance, you can print out the guest's name and table number on a small square of color-coordinated paper and slip it into a small silver frame.

If you have a larger crowd and need to number the guests' tables, borrow this idea from Robyn in New York, whose bridesmaids used fun eight-by-ten pictures of Robyn striking different poses while holding up a big sign with each number on it. This cute touch personalized the centerpieces and tickled the guests.

Give each table a name instead of a number, and make the names work with the themes. For the Moon and Stars shower, for instance, you might seat your guests at tables named after planets or constellations. Be creative, and decorate the table place cards with stickers, pictures, or drawings that go with the theme.

For an added touch to printouts of table names, frame them in colored picture frames. You can find fabulous frames—either classic silver or in fun, colorful, and theme-related styles—at camera shops, gift stores, and through the Web site www.exposures.com.

For your guests' dining and drinking pleasure, you can use your computer to print menu and wine list cards on card stock (matching the color and theme of the party, of course). Even at a buffet, the guests might like to read about the offerings waiting for them.

As a decorative and meaningful touch of decor on the dining, buffet, and cake tables, and even around the room, print several poems or quotes about love and marriage on decorative card stock. One bridal party in Kentucky told me they printed out in swirly computer font a saying from Anne Morrow Lindbergh that was very special to the bride.

Use your computer to print out game cards, surveys, questionnaires, and any other printed items you'll need for games. It's easy to slip index cards into the envelope slot of your printer, and it's a lot easier than writing them by hand.

For game cards, use colored index cards, which you can get in bulk quite inexpensively at office supply stores. I've seen pastel colors, brights, fluorescents, and even index cards printed with designs on them. You can get unlined index cards if that works better for your game-card design.

Use theme-oriented stickers to decorate the game cards you've printed out on index cards. Children can help out with this task.

Name tags are often a very good idea at showers where half the guests may not know the other half. You can have guests write out their own name tags, or you can do them beforehand in fancy handwriting or computer font.

A great touch for shower name tags, if you're writing them out yourself, is to identify guests by their relation to the bride. You might put "Tracy, Maid of Honor," "Amanda, bride's college roommate and friend for 20

years," or "Wendy, bride's boss." These name tags are instant icebreakers, giving guests a quick way to relate to one another. Use these icebreaker name tags at co-ed showers to which a lot of single men and women are invited. You don't have to put their astrological signs on them, of course (or, as one single bridesmaid requested, a secret symbol that tells all the women a certain handsome male guest is a "'commitment-phobic player" so stay away!)—just names and relation to the bride and groom.

While they're usually reserved for weddings, printed napkins and matchbooks can also be a part of your big day. Check at party stores, custom-printing houses, and bridal and party supply catalogs and Web sites.

Decor That Moves!

Set up a television in the corner of the room and run a video or DVD showing footage that relates to the shower's theme. For instance, you might play a performance of a jazz band in keeping with the New Orleans theme, hula dances for your luau, or classic television shows and old MTV footage to match your '80s theme.

Get out those videotapes from the bride's younger days, perhaps that video you shot of the girls at the karaoke bar, old footage from your college homecoming tailgate parties, footage from your best years together.

For a sports-themed shower, run videos of some of the guys' endless footage of college or pro-football games.

Turn down the sound and just have the visuals running in the background on one or several televisions.

◆

Can't find video footage that suits your theme? Then shoot it yourself! Gather some friends together weeks before the shower, set up your trusty camcorder on a tripod, and shoot yourselves all dressed up, with props to match your theme. You might all dress and act like a throng of paparazzi lined up behind a velvet rope, holding up your cameras and shouting to the guests (viewers) to pose for a picture, as fitting for the Oscar-night shower or the diva shower.

◆

Make the guests part of the color scheme. If you ask all your guests to dress in white, red, floral, or any color of your choosing, they become a part of the color palette and coordinate with the room. Then the bride stands out in the crowd and it makes for great group pictures!

◆

You'll find more ideas for appropriate room and table decor in the theme showers in chapters 12 and 13.

Entertainment
and Games

So now you have a beautifully decorated room and a delicious food and drink menu all planned. That means you're halfway to your goal of creating a fabulous bridal shower! Time to figure out which shower games will get your guests laughing, dancing, and delighting the guest(s) of honor.

Don't worry, you're going far from (or adding a new fun twist to) those tired old traditional games that everyone has played at every shower they've ever been to (Clothespins, anyone?). No more groaning and eye rolling when a way-too-chipper host announces the arrival of Enforced Fun Time. You're going to get much more original. From the silly to the sentimental, the traditional to the trendy, these planned activities are sure to be the hit of the party!

Music

Before you call out "Let the games begin!" it's a great idea to have some form of entertainment in action throughout the earlier, more subdued portion of the party. That might be soft music playing in the background, or theme music that matches the style of the party.

Create a personalized mix of songs to play throughout the shower. Label one CD for softer tunes during the meal, and then pop in another CD loaded with more festive songs. Use a theme for your party's soundtrack, or just record songs that have a lot of meaning for the bride, groom, their group of friends, or their family.

It's great entertainment when a group of the bride's guests get together to sing a song karaoke-style, either along with a stereo sound system or with an actual karaoke machine. No, you don't have to rent an expensive soundboard and video monitor for the sing-along. Do as others have done and borrow a friend's system, hook a microphone into a laptop logged into a karaoke Web site, or use an inexpensive children's karaoke machine, which you can find at a toy store.

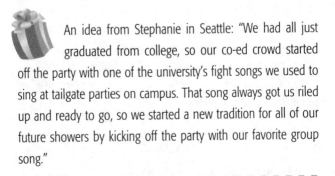

An idea from Stephanie in Seattle: "We had all just graduated from college, so our co-ed crowd started off the party with one of the university's fight songs we used to sing at tailgate parties on campus. That song always got us riled up and ready to go, so we started a new tradition for all of our future showers by kicking off the party with our favorite group song."

Let the Games Begin!

Let's hope you have a fun-loving crowd on your guest list, because it's the truly good-natured who will make the most of original shower games. A good rule of thumb for any shower—especially when you have a mixed crowd of guests with some who are "game" and others who are "lame"—is to make participation *optional*. Those who wish to play can stay, and those who wish to opt out can move into another room for cocktails, or onto the terrace for continued mingling time. Or they can sit on the sidelines and enjoy the show, which they'll appreciate being free to do. Some people are observers in life, and they too should be made comfortable at the party.

Obviously, keep taste in mind when designing the game portion of the shower, especially if the bride is concerned about what her future mother-in-law thinks of her and of the people she knows. The more raunchy party games can be saved for the bachelorette party.

And now, here are some fun games to get your crowd laughing, and perhaps the bride (and groom, if you're going co-ed!) blushing . . .

The Clothespin Game

I know, I know, I said I was going to take you away from the tired, old games of years past, but I've added a few little twists to make this game a bit more "now."

◆

The Clothespin Game is probably best known and most often played at showers across the country. Each guest is given several clothespins (five is a good number) to attach to their clothing. The leader of the game announces that a certain word or phrase is taboo for the first hour of the party, and if one guest hears another guest utter the dreaded word or phrase, she then takes one of the offender's clothespins and attaches it to her own outfit. The guest with the most clothespins at the end of the game wins the prize.

◆

Some common taboo words are: gorgeous, beautiful, pretty, wedding, present(s) or gift(s), great (guests are commonly "nabbed" on this one in answering the sly question, "How are the kids doing?"), the bride's name, the groom's name, some element of the room, hi, or hello. Some of the more devious shower hosts I've spoken to made the buzzword any name of any person in the room.

◆

The buzzword doesn't have to be a word. It can be a gesture: pointing, touching your face or earring, crossing your legs (try *not* doing that all afternoon!), sitting sideways in your chair, or touching someone for emphasis when you speak. Choose a common gesture and watch those clothespins changing hands like crazy.

What's in Your Purse?

This too is an often-played game, but I have a few twists for you. The key to this one is printing out a checklist of 20 or so items that are commonly found in a woman's pocketbook or purse. Each guest receives this checklist and marks off each item she actually has in her purse at that moment. More uncommon items can be given extra points to add to the winner's total score. Here are some items to put on your checklist of purse contents:

One group of fun-loving shower hosts from Delaware shared a twist on a college drinking game that worked well for the clothespin game (minus the flaming shots of liquor, of course!). Before anyone takes a sip of their drink, they have to say or shout out a phrase, such as "I love bridal showers!" or "Good luck to the bride and groom!" The options for these phrases are endless—they can be wacky ("I just love a good piece of cheese-cake in the morning"), racy ("I haven't had sex in a week!"), or complimentary ("Hey, [bride's name], you look amazing today!").

Do your group a favor and limit the time of this game, because it's a riot for a short time, but then it just gets annoying.

$10 bill
$20 bill
$50 bill
$100 bill
Nothing but singles
No cash at all
Subway token
Checkbook
Driver's license
More than three credit cards
MAC card
Library card
Gym membership card
Breath mints
Chewing gum
Lipstick
Eyeliner

Powder compact
Tissues
Tweezers
Mirror
Pen
Hairbrush or comb
Cell phone
PDA
Picture of a child
Picture of a spouse or sweetheart
Advil, Motrin, or other pain reliever
Tampon or other feminine care product
Postage stamp
Business card
Address book

◆

Some Extra-Credit Items

Condom

Foreign coin or paper
money

Book

Lucky charm (rabbit's
foot, lucky medallion,
crystal, feng shui
talisman)

Someone's phone num-
ber written on a napkin

Chewed piece of gum
wrapped in paper

Asthma inhaler

Birth control pills

Picture of the bride

Driver's license with no
photo on it (yes, they
do give these out)

Learner's permit (for
younger guests)

◆

For the twist I promised, you can make the prize go to the person with the *least* amount of points, rather than the most—just for lightening her load and taking it easy on her back every day. The guests will never be expecting that!

◆

A second prize can go to the person with the most unusual item in her purse. The crowd votes by applause for each item. A prize can go to the one who has the most pictures of their children, nieces, nephews, and others.

◆

Another twist: Use the bathroom scale to weigh everyone's full purses. The winner can be the one with the heaviest or the lightest bag—your choice. If the award goes to the owner of the heaviest bag, the prize might be a gift certificate for a massage to unkink her tired shoulders.

What's in Your Wallet?

Let's not leave the men out of this one! At a co-ed shower, both men and women can whip out their wallets for a little competition. Besides, if at this party all the women are scavenging through their purses, how much fun would it be if the men were all standing around snickering at "all the junk women carry around"? The checklist printout for wallet contents might include:

$10 bill

$20 bill

$50 bill

$100 bill

Nothing but singles

No cash at all

Driver's license

More than three credit cards

Library card

Gym membership card

Business card

Someone else's business card (an extra point for each one)

Picture of a sweetheart or spouse

Picture of a child

Frequent shopper card with holes punched for each visit

Attached checkbook

Pen

Condom

More than one condom

Someone's number written on a napkin or business card

◆

Again, the winner might have the most or least points totaled, and an extra prize can be given to the person with the most unusual item, the most pictures of their child, the most numbers written in lipstick on napkins and business cards, and so forth.

Search for Kisses

Before the party, hide the contents of a few bags of Hershey's Kisses around the room—in centerpieces, on the buffet table, on window ledges, in planters, in the restroom, behind the gifts, and so on—and then announce that the guest who finds the most Kisses wins a prize. Watch your guests scatter in search of these sweet treats.

◆

A twist on this game: Use candies with relevant names, such as Almond *Joy*. Or go for an interesting theme shape of Gummi candy, but in accordance with the party's theme. Check your local party supply or candy store for some unique ideas.

The Bride and Groom Quiz

How well does everyone know the bride and groom? Test their knowledge with a little quiz you've written up about both of them and their history as a couple. To make it easy on guests, make it no more than 20 questions, and make it multiple choice. A few ideas might be:

1. **Where did Jennifer and Steve first meet?**
   a) at a Homecoming dance in college
   b) in a bar
   c) in prison

2. **Where did Steve propose to Jennifer?**
   a) on the beach at sunset in Cape Cod
   b) on the beach at sunset in Newport
   c) on the beach at sunrise on Martha's Vineyard

3. **What was Jennifer's nickname for Steve after their first date?**
   a) Mr. Hands
   b) Hottie McHot Hot
   c) Steve who?

4. **When does Steve say he first fell in love with Jennifer?**
   a) after their second date
   b) when she bailed him out of jail
   c) when he saw her playing with his niece and nephew

This can be a really fun game, with off-the-wall answers that will tickle the bride and groom with reminders of their best moments together. After the guests fill out their quizzes, grab an "accountant" friend to tally the results against the real answers on your master sheet and announce the winner(s).

Dear Diary

This game takes some preparation time and a bit of creative writing, but it's a fun presentation for the bride and groom. With the guests well fed and perhaps floating a bit on their cocktails, the host gathers everyone around to hear entries from the bride's and groom's diaries. Of course, these are made-up diaries that you've written, giving fake versions of what the bride and groom wrote after their first date, their first kiss, meeting each other's families, their first "intimate moment," getting engaged, and so on. You then hand the bride "her" diary and the groom "his" diary and ask them to read their entries to the group. (Of course, don't be too much of a devil in what you write, as you don't want to hit a sensitive nerve with anyone!) As the guests of honor spill out their fictional private thoughts, everyone, including them, will have a blast. Here's a sample of fake diary entries:

> **Bride:** Tonight was my first date with Kevin. I tried not to dress too sexy, since I'd heard he's very conservative and afraid of women who are too sensual.

(Laughs all around, since Kevin is known for liking his women in leopard-print teddies.)

Groom: First date with Tricia. Nice butt. Great lips. Doesn't talk much, though.

(Laughs all around, since Tricia is known for being chatty.)

Bride: Oh . . . my . . . God. Kevin finally kissed me, and it was the most incredible kiss I've ever experienced.

(Audience: "Awwwww!")

Groom: First night spent with Tricia, and it was so great I'm not even talking to my friends about it. How can I get this girl to only want to be with me for the rest of our lives?

Bride: First night spent with Kevin. How can I get this guy to only want to be with me for the rest of our lives?

Groom: Asked Tricia's Dad for her hand in marriage. I only had to give him $50 for him to say yes . . . that, and I had to promise we'd name the first kid after him.

I See a House in Your Future

This is a chain story. Guests take turns saying one sentence each to form a story that predicts the bride and groom's future life together. You can go around the room in order, or appoint a conductor to select who goes next. For instance:

Guest #1: "In the year 2007, Tricia discovers that she is pregnant. Steve is overjoyed and immediately begins building a . . ."

Guest #2: "Bigger stock portfolio. Do you know how much college will cost in 2025?! But soon, their money troubles are behind them when a very pregnant Tricia . . ."

Guest #3: "Wins $85 million in the Powerball lottery . . ."

Surveying the Future

Instead of telling a story about the bride and groom's future, survey the guests. At the outset of the party, hand out a questionnaire that asks the guests for their predictions about the couple's life together. Make it multiple choice, so that an "accountant" can tally the percentages ("Seventy-five percent of shower guests say that Maggie and Andrew will have a child in less than two years after the wedding. Twenty percent say three to five years, and five percent say Maggie's going to secretly destroy their birth control on the wedding night.").

My Advice to You

Guests receive index cards at the beginning of the party and are asked to record their best marriage advice on them and sign their names at the bottom of the card. The leader of this presentation can either read the advice along with the person's name, or ask the crowd to guess who contributed this little gem: "The key to a long and lasting marriage is wearing socks to bed. Cold feet under the covers means a cold romantic life."

Vow No-No's

Guests can use index cards to write down what *not* to say during the vows, making the entries all in good fun and as wacky as possible. For instance, "Do NOT promise to obey each other, because that's just not going to happen." Or you can go the other way and have guests say what the couple should include in their vows, such as "I promise to be true to you and honest with you, except for when you ask me if I think Derek Jeter is hotter than you," or "I promise to honor you, cherish you, be your best friend in good times and bad, and always pick up my wet towel from the bathroom floor."

How We Got Him to Propose
All in good fun, each guest takes turns spinning a tall tale about what he or she did or said to convince the groom to pop the question. Guests who've played along with this game have made up some whoppers about various bribes, promises, and blackmail.

How We Got the Bride to Say Yes
Once everyone has had fun with the groom's intentions, it's time for the guests to say how they convinced the bride to accept the groom's proposal of marriage. Again, bring out the tall tales, bribes, blackmail, and inside jokes.

When Will They Kiss?
It's just like the Superbowl pool at work, where guests enter their names in boxes on a chart, guessing the exact time that the bride and groom will kiss each other for the first time during the party. Of course, the guests of honor don't know this betting is going on. To make the chart, create a graph by blocking off 10- or 15-minute increments of the time allotted for the party. Each guest "claims" his or her time. When the couple kisses, cheers will erupt and the winner gets a prize.

Little Known Facts About the Bride and Groom
Guests can either write down or say the little-known facts that they possess about the bride and groom. They

might include favorite things of the bride and groom when they were kids, awards the bride won as a child, the groom's hidden talent for guitar playing, and lessons the guest learned from the happy couple.

Bridal Jeopardy
Set it up just like the game on television, only all the questions are about the bride and groom, their interests, careers, travels, and past experiences. Use a buzzer or bike horn for contestants to ring in with their answer.

Bridal Survivor
Just like the show on television, divide your guests into two "tribes"—and have fun naming them!—to compete in various skill and eating contests. Losing teams vote off one member at a time until the player who outlasts all becomes the ultimate survivor. Skill challenges might be a bit more appropriate (and less strenuous) than running an obstacle course on a deserted island. Instead, have guests tie a cherry stem with their tongue, do a children's puzzle, program the VCR to record *Friends*, or arrange music CDs in chronological order of their release. Food challenges might include eating a unique piece of sushi or drinking a strangely colored milkshake.

To Symbolize the Sweetness of Marriage
Fill a bag or box with an assortment of household items, toys, tools, foods, or cosmetics. Players each choose one item, hold it up to the crowd, and say what aspect of marriage that item symbolizes. Some suggestions:

> "This rolling pin symbolizes how the couple will smooth over all the rough spots in their marriage."

> "This cell phone symbolizes how the couple will always stay in close contact and have good communication, taking any opportunity to say 'I Love You.'"

"This egg timer symbolizes that life is short, so fill
it with as many happy moments as possible."

Name That Movie

Guests can either use their own favorite lines from
movies or choose pre-printed cards that you or a movie-
buff friend have written out. The game is to match the
famous movie quote with the title of the film. You can
use some obvious ones: "Frankly, my dear, I don't give
a damn," or go to a more difficult level. To find thousands of movie quotes from popular films, go to
www.movie quotes.com and search by the movie's title
for all the game entries you'll need. Here is a sample:

Quotes:
A. "I'll have what she's having."
B. "I feel the need . . . the need for speed."
C. "Would you care for a roll in zee hay?"
D. "Ease his pain."
E. "You work on commission, don't you? Big mis-
take! Big! Huge!"

Answers:
A. *When Harry Met Sally*
B. *Top Gun*
C. *Young Frankenstein*
D. *Field of Dreams*
E. *Pretty Woman*

Who's Been Hitched the Longest?

All players have to guess who in the room has been
with their current partner for the longest amount of
time. The people who guess correctly and the longest-
hitched person (or people) get prizes.

Marriage Mad Libs

You know those Mad Lib pads you've seen in stores, and you probably filled them out when you were a kid. (If you don't know, Mad Libs are a fill-in-the-blank word game where players are asked for any noun, verb, adverb, person's name, etc. and these words are filled into the text of a running story. When the story is read aloud, those random words plugged into the narrative can be quite amusing . . . such as: One *cold* August night, a *cable guy* and an *FBI agent* were flying to *Detroit* to attend the opening of a *mashed potato* museum.) Now, you can find wedding-themed Mad Lib booklets in party stores for your group to play with. If you can't find them and have a little extra time, print out your own on your computer.

If It Has "Love" in the Title

All players have to list every song they can think of with the word "love" in the title. The person with the most titles wins. As a fun twist, try a different word, perhaps one that works with the party's theme, such as "beach," "ocean," or "dance."

Guess the Magic Number

Fill a fish bowl with candies, golf balls, or any other small object that fits your shower theme (count the objects before you put them in). Then ask your guests to record on paper their "guesstimates" of the number to see who comes closest to the grand total. Be creative with what you put in the bowl. Some themes open up great options, such as a bowl full of Mardi-Gras bead necklaces, seashells, or poker chips or crumpled play money for that Vegas-night theme.

You're No Tiger Woods, Baby!

Grab a few putters and some golf balls, and then create your own mini–golf course in the room for the guests to play through. You can create fabulous obstacles using plastic cups, children's toys, garden hoses, what have you. You might even make a staircase part of the fun, with guests having to hit the ball down into a cup on a certain step or at the bottom of the stairs. Shoot through a tunnel made out of chairs, around a corner, past potted plants, and over a tricky tile floor.

How Many Great Lovers Can You Name?

No, not your own! We're talking about great lovers throughout history and in literature, entertainment, and movies. Romeo and Juliet, Elizabeth Barrett Browning and Robert Browning, George Burns and Gracie Allen. Ask your guests to write down as many famous real-life or fictional loves they can name, and the winner gets a prize.

Work Your Theme

Chapters 12 and 13 provide more games related to specific themed showers. With your creativity humming from the above ideas, you can come up with personalized twists on games that will be perfect for your crowd and theme. If you go with a unique idea and match it to your crowd's age and fun-quotient, your shower is sure to be a laugh-out-loud fun-fest and a big success all around.

Opening the Gifts

For the bride, opening all those beautifully wrapped shower gifts is a highlight of the day, but did you know you can make the unwrapping session even better for both the bride *and* the guests? Brides with large guest lists can get a lot of presents, and especially if a fuss is made over each one, the unwrapping session can literally last for hours. The following are tips for the gift-opening process and ideas for making this sometimes long stretch of the shower more enjoyable for the bride and keeping the guests from slipping into a boredom coma.

Before the bows go flying, enlist a fellow shower host to help out by recording which guest gave which gift, as an aid for the bride when she writes her thank you's. The easiest way is to identify the present right on the guest's greeting card, rather than write the name and the gift on a separate pad. If the bride wishes to keep her cards as mementos and doesn't want anyone writing on them, record the gift on a Post-It note and stick it on the inside of the card.

Tradition has it that the shower hosts collect all the gift bows and ribbons and create a faux bridal bouquet for use at the rehearsal. Make sure your volunteers are stocked with a sturdy paper plate to serve as the base for the bouquet and plenty of tape for attaching the bows and ribbon.

Here's a fun twist on the old *bow*quet. Before the party, purchase a selection of bows and ribbons and attach them to a set of bra and panties, plus a set of boxers for the groom. Stash these masterpieces aside during the party, and then pull them out at the end or opening ceremony with a big "Ta da!" as an extra laugh for your guests and a present for the bride in addition to the on-the-spot bow bouquet creation.

Here's a common game at bridal showers: Unbeknownst to the bride, someone is writing down everything she says as she opens her gifts. All those "oooohs," "aahh-hhs," and "Yes! This is perfect!" statements are then read back to the bride and her crowd as what the bride is going to say on her wedding night. It's one of the oldest shower games in the book, so it needs a little twist to make it fresh. Rather than say that this is what the *bride* will say on the wedding night, make it what the *groom* will say. Or, make it what the groom said the first time he saw the bride naked (or the bride when she saw the groom naked—take your pick), which makes the phrase "And there are *three* of them!" very interesting. If the recorder isn't getting any good quotes from the bride, get her talking. Wise shower hosts know just the right questions to ask to guide the bride's comments. At a recent shower, one bridesmaid asked, "Are you having trouble getting the gift out of the box, Sheryl?" And Sheryl innocently delivered a gem for the list: "Let me just twist this and it will slide right out!"

If the guest list is large and you expect that it will take a *looooong* time for the bride to get through the gifts, then do everyone a favor and split up the gift-opening session. The bride opens a dozen or so right after the meal, then everyone has cake; then she opens a dozen more, and then you play a game; and so on. Breaking it up is a welcome relief for everyone, as guests don't have to squirm in their seats for hours and the bride gets a break from all that gift opening.

If there aren't too many gifts on the table, then it may be enough to have the cake and coffee served to the guests while the bride is opening her presents. That caffeine can perk them up a bit for the ride home or for any games you have planned as a shower closer.

Incorporate a fun shower game into the opening of the gifts. Grab a kitchen timer and set it for 10 minutes when the bride starts opening her gifts. When the timer dings, the guest whose gift the bride is holding gets a prize of her own (see chapter 11 for prize ideas).

To add a surprise for guests and a little extra zing to the opening process, all gifts with a bow of a certain color (pink or iridescent, for instance) win a small prize for the giver. Call it a reward for being a little more creative than the standard white bow.

Add in a prize for the most attractively wrapped present. Whether you alert guests ahead of time about this contest is up to you!

Throw in a gag gift every now and then from a special section where you've stowed them apart from the real gifts. The look on the bride's face when she opens something completely off the wall, such as an Etch-a-Sketch toy, a how-to erotic massage video, or a Power-puff girl's lunch box, will be priceless.

Smart hosts can tell when the guests are drifting off into those boredom comas, so here's a trick to perk them up. Make those small gag gifts easily identifiable; wrap them all in bright purple paper, for instance. When the guests see that purple gift coming off the endless presents table, they'll perk up, knowing something fun is about to happen. Ham it up while you're handing it over, too. It's all in good fun.

Let kids participate in the opening process. The flower girl can take off the bows, for instance, and hand them to the crafty host making the faux bouquet.

Here's a hint from brides who have had the children assist with the unwrapping: afterwards, give each child a nice present of her own for being so helpful.

Make post-party cleanup easier by assigning a fellow host to act as "trashmaster," stuffing torn wrapping paper into a big plastic bag or garbage container as the bride opens the presents. Ask the trashmaster not to throw out pretty gift bags. They can be given to the bride for her own use later, or for carrying home smaller gifts or "wishing well" presents, if you've asked guests to bring those. By the way, the bride doesn't have to go through all of the wishing well gifts and show them to the crowd. Spices and cotton balls aren't that exciting.

Make it easy for the bride to get her loot home. You might bring along an empty suitcase on wheels, a dolly, or a luggage pull cart to help transport everything to the car.

Touching Tributes

For the most touching and memorable of showers, sometimes it's not the games you play or the gifts you display, but the words you say that can make even the most modest bridal shower priceless.

As host, think about incorporating some well-timed tributes and toasts into your celebration. Use the more laid-back tone of the party and the receptive audience of the bride's closest girlfriends, family, and colleagues as the perfect setting to speak freely and generously about the guest (or guests) of honor in a way that the wedding day probably won't allow you to do. Now is the time and this is the place, so get ready to take center stage, even if only for a short and sweet presentation.

Your Opening Remarks

Open the party by getting everyone's attention right at the start. Explain who you are in relation to the bride, as in "Hannah and I have known each other for 23 years.

- -

Some Rules About Toasts and Tributes During Bridal Showers

1. Keep it short and simple. Rambling speeches are not the way to start the party.

2. Use humor, because laughter is the best way to get things rolling.

3. Know what you're going to say. Winging it invites Spotlight Freeze and your rambling presentation can be awkward and embarrassing for all.

4. Make it personal to the bride, not a rehearsed Hallmark card sentiment.

5. Stay away from the too-personal stuff, such as the time you helped the bride overcome her depression during college. No one needs to know that, even if you have the best intentions.

6. Share the spotlight with others who wish to toast the bride and groom.

7. Let the guests know from the start that this is going to be a unique and fabulous party they'll never forget.

- -

We were college roommates, we grew up together, and she's like a sister to me."

Speak personally about the bride's best traits, how confident you are that she's going to be a magnificent wife (and someday, mother) and how she deserves the best future possible with the love of her life.

Share some of your favorite memories of the bride in order to convey to the guests a real sense of who the bride is. Make them funny, touching, sentimental—talk about how the bride came through for you during a difficult time, and how she deserves only the best in life. Remember, some of the women (and men) in attendance may not know her too well, so this introduction of yours may actually be their first impression of her. Not too much pressure on you, is it?

Assure the guests that this isn't going to be your average run-of-the-mill bridal shower. Tell them you have some fun surprises in store, that you'll be doing things a little differently from what they might expect, and that they should prepare themselves for a shower unlike any other. Your initial announcement could lift everyone's expectations for the event ahead.

The Kindest Words

Allow the bride to stand, accompanied by applause from her guests, of course, and invite her to say a few words (she may thank her guests for coming and express how much she's looking forward to the afternoon/evening ahead). Giving the bride the floor is a great opener to the party. She might be relaxed, she might be emotional, she might still be in a bit of shock; her words will come right from the heart and will be remembered forever as her real response to the surprise event.

Share the stage. Throughout the event, invite key guests to make a brief tribute of their choice. Be sure to scatter these throughout the party so it doesn't come off as a corporate lecture with an endless lineup of droning speakers. Here are some key people you might want to call upon to speak:

The bride's mother (parents)

The groom's mother (parents)

The maid of honor

The bridesmaids

The bride's sisters (brothers)

The bride's grandmother, godmother, or special aunts and cousins (male relatives if a co-ed shower)

The couple who introduced the bride and groom

◆

For extra luck for the wedding and the marriage ahead, ask the longest-married woman or couple in the room to say a few words.

◆

When others agree to speak or make a toast, they should be free to give an off-the-cuff, spontaneous toast, read a favorite poem, dedicate a song, share a favorite memory, or even just say a few words and hug the bride.

Creative and Surprise Tributes

Rather than repeat a cookie-cutter best-wishes toast (as touching as the most practiced wording can be), have a little fun with it. Delight your guest with a Letterman-like Top 10 list of why the bride is going to have a wonderful marriage, or why the groom is lucky to have "landed" her.

♥

If children are included in the bridal party, have the kids propose a toast with their apple juice, punch, or soda. Out of the mouths of babes can come the funniest, hammiest, and even the most truth-laced tribute of the day.

♥

Produce a cameo. No, not your grandmother's brooch, but rather a cameo surprise appearance by a very special friend of the bride's whom no one thought could fly in to attend. Make the surprise a creative one by blindfolding the bride and letting her perhaps jet-lagged friend begin her tribute from another room (over a microphone, if you have one), with the bride left to tear off her blindfold with a thrilled squeal and run to embrace her good friend. Now that's an unexpected tribute.

♥

Include guests who couldn't come to the shower by reading aloud their mailed, e-mailed, or telegrammed good wishes, explaining to the crowd how the kind friend, relative, or colleague is related to the bride. This is great if health or distance keeps a truly special guest, such as the bride's mother, from attending.

♥

Who knew that Sting, First Lady Laura Bush, Sammy Sosa, and the cast of *Friends* couldn't make the trip to the party? As a fun addition to the reading of messages, write some fake cards and all-in-good-fun wishes from the bride and groom's favorite celebrities. Make it wild, make it overflow with inside jokes, make everyone smile. Have a blast with this one, but keep it limited for time's sake.

♥

Wheel out the VCR and TV to run a congratulations videotape, featuring toasts and tributes from those who couldn't attend the party or from the groom, parents or other relatives, longtime friends, groups of good friends, or work colleagues. Keep the video short (under 15 minutes) for the sake of the party's flow and your guests' attention spans.

♥

Put a fun and creative twist on the congratulations videotape by asking—well ahead of the party—helpers who have access to well-known personalities to videotape them giving a VIP message to the bride. One bride from New York City told me that she had regular access to sports personalities through her job as an agent's assistant. In stolen moments, she recorded short personal greetings from the groom's current sports heroes, which thrilled both bride and groom. For a bride who had a lifelong fantasy about firefighters, several of her friends actually stopped in at firehouses across their city and asked the firefighters to record short greetings to the bride. Big success!

♥

For a group with a wild-and-crazy sense of humor, before the party, tape willing strangers (with their permission, of course) offering their congratulations to the happy couple. They might be handsome Wall Street types loosened up at happy hour, lifeguards at the beach, or even the local high school's cheerleading team doing a special cheer for the bride and groom. Use your creativity and contacts and edit a unique and original tribute videotape to kick off the party.

Give the groom his own spotlight with a three-minute video greeting to his bride and the roomful of ladies, showing his love for his future wife and his romantic side for all to admire.

Say It with Music

Bring fond memories to the party by playing the bride's favorite songs.

Make up a badly rhymed and goofy song filled with in-side jokes and giggles for all (like something Phoebe from *Friends* would perform!), ending with a more serious wish for a long and happy marriage, future, and all of the couple's dreams to come true.

Allow the Bride the Last Word

At the end of the party, invite the bride to speak once again, from the heart, about what this shower has meant to her and what it's meant to have all of her most-cherished people there to share it with her. The last word sometimes holds the sweetest sentiments and is the finest way to end the bride's party on a perfect note.

If the party is co-ed, the bride and groom might decide to propose toasts and give tributes to one another as well. These might be funny, sentimental, a mutual volley of their Top 10 lists about one another, or just a short and sweet "I love you," sealed with a kiss.

11

Favors and Prizes

Since the same types of items work as both favors and game prizes, I've bunched them all together here for you to pick and choose those you prefer. Some speak for themselves (silver picture frames, for instance) and some call for a little more detail (gift books and gift certificates). Before we get to the list, I want to remind you of the best places to shop for these gift items:

Craft stores. You can find everything from silver frames to candleholders and potpourri bowls at a huge discount over gift shops, and you may be able to get further price cuts on bulk buys.

Party supply stores. Naturally, this type of store provides aisles and aisles of cute, theme-oriented items that are perfect for favors and gifts.

Bookstores. Little gift books, calendars, frames, music CDs, and collections of essays are all found here, in addition to fun gift items such as magnetic poetry sets, temporary word tattoos, and bookmarks.

Dollar stores. For gag gifts, candles, frames, and potpourri, the dollar store is an inexpensive source for game prizes.

Candy stores. Whether it's a custom-made chocolate shop or a bulk candy shop with bins and big shovels for scooping out jelly beans, the candy store is a great place to load up on confections and gift containers to hold them.

Liquor stores. These are not just for bottles of wine as favors, but for smaller bottles of liqueurs, wine enthusiast supplies (such as books, magazines, wine charms, and cork stoppers), and gourmet snacks and goodies.

Catalogs. You might find some favors and gifts under $5 to buy en masse, as well as those pricier specialty items that are perfect for your party's theme.

Favor and gift Web sites. Many gift and specialty catalogs have an associated Web site, but be sure to check out www.beau-coup.com, one of my favorite sources for beautiful, elegant, and inexpensive favors and gift items.

Edible Favors

Godiva chocolates. From raspberry-filled starfish shapes to key lime truffles and chocolate in theme-appropriate forms, Godiva is the gold standard of edible party favorites.

◆

Homemade chocolates. You can get them at a candy shop or make them yourself using melted chocolate and candy form trays, adding sticks to turn your creations into chocolate lollipops. Craft stores carry candy form trays in a host of theme shapes: beach (starfish, seahorses, and beach balls), hearts, wedding, winter (snowflakes and snowmen), flowers, and so on. Purchase tinted chocolate to make your home-melted favors conform to your theme.

◆

Chocolate roses. Wrap the ends in color-coordinated foil.

◆

Fortune cookies. Buy these in bulk at an Asian market, or make your own. For a little extra flair, dip half of each cookie in melted chocolate and dust with colored or theme-appropriate edible baking sprinkles. Gourmet shops sell sprinkles in the shape of hearts, snowflakes, balloons, fish, and more.

◆

Chocolate-covered everything. Dip strawberries, dried apricots, cherries, peanuts, cookies, pretzels, and even coffee stirrers and spoons into melted form chocolate and then let them solidify on wax paper before packaging as favors. To get the best results, use a specifically packaged mix for dipping strawberries (found in gourmet shops and supermarkets).

◆

Sugared almonds (or dragées). In white or pastel shades, these are the traditional bridal gift.

◆

Petit fours. These little frosted cakes are another traditional choice among the bridal set. Like mini–wedding cakes, they might be filled with strawberry, chocolate, or whipped cream and iced with pastel or white frosting, with a mini-rose piped on top. Box them individually in plastic boxes for the best presentation.

◆

Jelly beans or miniature candy bars. Put them in bags, boxes, or tins.

◆

Brownies. Dress them up with themed sprinkles or frosting or use a cookie cutter to shape them into stars, hearts, or other theme-oriented shapes; package individually.

◆

Sugar cookies. Make them yourself or use a pre-packaged sugar-cookie dough. Cut them with a theme-oriented cookie cutter, frost with a thin layer of colored icing, and pipe on designs with white icing.

◆

Chocolate-chip cookies. Bake yourself or let Mrs. Fields do it for you in a variety of flavors.

Meringue cookies. Get a great recipe and pipe out these white or pastel-colored clouds to harden and serve.

Drink-mix baskets. Fill a basket with two margarita glasses, a little margarita recipe book, a pair of sunglasses, and a beach-read novel; or make it a martini basket with two fun-shaped martini glasses and a recipe book or martini boxed-card recipe set.

Tea basket. Fill a basket with a beautiful or fun-message teacup, a selection of packaged tea bags (try the Tazo sampler at Starbucks), some individually wrapped cookies or sugar wafers, and a great paperback novel.

Personalized wine or beer bottles. Create the labels yourself using your home computer and printer, and then just stick your custom label on each bottle. (Tip: put each label on the *back* of the bottle, since guests might want to read the original label for vineyard info, ingredients list for allergies, and so forth.)

Mood-Setting Favors

Candles. Choose from an enormous variety of shapes, colors, scents, and sizes at a craft shop or at Illumi-nations.com. Add a pretty candleholder or candle tray to complete the gift.

Aromatherapy products. These can be candles, scent oils, lavender water bottles (for adding to the laundry when you're washing sheets and towels . . . Ahhhhh!), scented room mists, rub-on scents, and potpourri.

Pampering products. Fill mini-baskets with assorted pampering products, such as hand cream, cocoa butter lotion, oatmeal soap, nail polish, and salon-style hair products.

Massage basket. Fill a basket or tin with a selection of massage oils in several scents—vanilla, lavender, sandalwood, and jasmine are just a few romantic choices—and add a how-to book or video on couples massage, foot massage and reflexology charts, and a CD of relaxing music.

Music CDs. Select a variety of mood-enhancing music from soft jazz to instrumental to Native American. Pick your favorites or ask a store clerk to help you choose some unique selections.

Champagne baskets. Fill a basket with a bottle of champagne, two champagne glasses, and a small packet of fresh strawberries, which enhance the flavor of the drink.

Wines. Check www.winespectator.com for ideas on unique vintages and the latest top-rated wines on the market.

Single flowers. The most elegant and beautiful favor I ever received was a single freshly cut white gardenia set in a clear square plastic box, with silk greenery and just a bit of water added to the box to keep the flower moist—simply gorgeous. Another option is individually wrapped single roses, lilies, sunflowers, or a big bright Gerbera daisy.

Gift certificates for dinner or dessert. Choose a local romantic restaurant or lounge.

Favors with a Future

Picture frames (with or without a photo of you and the guest). Choose from silver frames, laser-cut wood frames, novelty frames in color and with decorations, the new "talking" frames with a computer chip that plays a song or a message in your own voice, or a frame on which you've engraved the person's name or a favorite quote.

Picture-feature gifts. If you have a great photo of the bride, or even a great photo that works with your theme (such as a shot of the Eiffel Tower or a sunset over the ocean), feature that photo in a keepsake favor or prize from www.shutterfly.com. This site will imprint your photo on anything from coffee mugs and coasters to magnets, T-shirts, calendars, and mouse pads.

Books. Choose from inspirational gift books, poetry collections, quote books, humor titles, books by a favorite author, recipe collections, or small illustration-oriented books that work with your theme, such as a book about flowers or seashells. Some of my favorites for book prizes or favors are:

Gift from the Sea by Anne Morrow Lindbergh

A Short Guide to a Happy Life by Anna Quindlen

The Prayer of Jabez by Bruce Wilkinson

The Everything Wine Book by Danny May and Andy Sharpe

Highballs, High Heels: A Girl's Guide to the Art of Cocktails by Karen Brooks, Gideon Bosker, and Reed Darmon

365 Ways to Relax Mind, Body, and Soul by Barbara Heller

Even God Is Single: So Stop Giving Me a Hard Time by Karen Salmansohn (Great for your single friends! This book is laugh-out-loud funny and empowering for the uncoupled friend or bridesmaid.)

◎

Bookmarks. Printed with theme-oriented illustrations such as the Eiffel Tower or a Tuscan vineyard, famous quotes or inspirational sayings such as Anais Nin's "Dreams are Necessary to Life," superheroes and children's book characters, flowers, sandcastles, and so on.

◎

Movie videos or DVDs. Connect these to your theme, such as romantic movies from the 1980s, and buy a wide variety so guests have a choice.

◎

Journals with pens. Check out both large and small specialty bookstores for a wide range of journals with decorative covers and inside quotes and messages.

Magnets with great sayings on them, such as "Life is either a daring adventure or nothing at all"—Helen Keller.

Key chains with attached famous quotes, pictures, or mini mirrors.

Coffee mugs with heartfelt messages on them. My absolute favorite is from Maya Angelou's line of gift items: "Only equals can be friends."

Travel decanters that keep coffee hot.

Music CDs.

Bumper stickers.

Calendars and date books.

Silver powder compacts.

Silver business card cases.

Silver treasure boxes.

Snowglobes.

Holiday ornaments. Shop on holiday weekends and after the holidays for especially good prices.

Potted flowering plants or seedlings. Guests can plant these and watch them grow for a season or forever. Here's a great tip for a truly useful potted plant that looks more expensive than it is. Buy rosemary seedlings that stand more than four inches tall and wrap the plain plastic holder with colored foil and a ribbon. Other herb options: get larger pots or baskets and transplant into each a selection of mint, rosemary, chives, parsley, or other herbs for a mini–kitchen garden.

Basket of seed packets with gardening gloves and a mini gardening book.

Wearable Favors

Charm bracelets.

Initial necklaces.

Good luck bead bracelets (such as the popular feng shui "love charm" bracelets and holistic jewelry at www.mjg designs.com).

◆

Toe rings.

◆

Mood rings.

◆

Ankle bracelets.

◆

Birthstone jewelry.

◆

Heart-locket necklaces or bracelets.

◆

Fake belly rings.

◆

Belly chains.

◆

Temporary tattoos. Go with words and phrases (found at the bookstore in such themes as "Romantic" and "Literary") or match the tattoos to your party's theme! Craft stores stock a wide variety of temporary skin art designs from Harley Davidson designs to the Powerpuff Girls.

◆

Tiaras and other hair accessories. Get fun-colored styles at accessory shops where the pre-teens go. Especially in the months before prom-time, you'll find a ton of great tiaras, jeweled hair clips, and ultra-flirty accessories to choose from.

◆

Imprinted, colored rubber-band bracelets with great sayings on them, as in, "My diamond bracelet is being cleaned."

◆

T-shirts with interesting quotes or graphics on them. Buy these from a gift catalog or make your own using graphic transfer paper and a computer printout, or use fabric pens to write a message or draw designs.

◆

Hats printed with fun messages.

◆

Fuzzy slippers.

◆

Robes. Go with a lightweight silk or satin in a pretty pastel color—or fire-engine red!

◆

Scarf and glove sets. Elegant neutrals or bright and playful blue leopard prints.

◆

Sunglasses. Choose elegant styles or bright colors.

◆

Nail polish sets. In wine colors, brights, and pastels, or playful sparkly or iridescent teen-type styles.

◆

Perfumes. Always a great gift, choose something new and original, or go with smaller bottles of a fine perfume. As an added plus, the perfume might work with your party's theme, such as "Sunflowers" or "Ocean Breeze."

Gift Certificates

Gift certificates make *great* favors and prizes, as the recipient gets to choose her own item or experience on an expense-free outing! Choose from the following types of gift certificates:

♥

Lingerie store.

♥

Bookstore.

♥

Music store.

♥

Video rental store.

♥

Movie theater.

❤

Coffee shop.

❤

Beauty salon or day spa.

❤

Local restaurant for brunch, lunch, dinner, drinks, or dessert.

❤

Local jazz club.

❤

Department store.

❤

Beauty supply store.

❤

Home decor store.

Gifts of Charity

Some hosts prefer to make a donation to charity in lieu of favors both at weddings and at bridal showers, especially if the bride or groom is active with a particular foundation or cause. If this is the way you want to go, create pretty announcement cards on your computer, print them on attractive card stock, and attach a little something to the card so the guests get a little treat as well. Here are some ideas for the treats:

◎

Foil-wrapped chocolate heart to accompany a donation to a heart foundation.

Pink ribbon pin to accompany a donation to the fight against breast cancer.

Small panda magnet to accompany a donation to the World Wildlife Federation.

Small starfish magnet or charm to accompany a donation to an oceanography institute.

Pack of mints as a "Breath of Fresh Air" to accompany a donation to the American Lung Association.

Framed rendition of the new firefighter heroes postage stamp to accompany a donation to any 9/11 organization or firefighters' widows and children's fund.

Baby picture of the bride to accompany a donation to the March of Dimes.

Small picture gift book on the chosen subject to accompany a donation to a "save the baby seals, whales, or spotted owls", for instance.

NOTE: You can check out any charity or foundation you're planning to donate to at www.give.org, a clearinghouse that publishes the ratings and legitimacy of established charities.

Favors for Co-ed Showers

The men are *not* likely to want a toe ring or a book of romantic poetry, so if your guest list is co-ed, choose favors and prizes friendly to both men and women from these possibilities:

◆

Bottles of wine.

◆

Bottles of liquor, such as brandy, cognac, Grand Marnier.

◆

Martini sets.

◆

Unique shot glasses or martini glasses.

◆

Cocktail shakers.

◆

Decorated coasters.

◆

Unique microbrew beers from different countries or states.

◆

Godiva chocolates.

◆

Picture frames.

◆

Silver business card cases.

◆

Music CDs.

◆

Movie videos or DVDs.

◆

Coffee mugs.

◆

Travel decanters.

◆

Gift certificates to coffee shops, music stores, movie
rental stores, movie theaters, restaurants, golf centers,
even beauty salons (for those haircuts, waxings, and
skin treatments that men don't admit they're getting!)

◆

Coffee baskets.

◆

Temporary tattoo sets.

◆

Key chains.

◆

Books and gift books, with a theme-oriented bookmark.

◆

Calendars and date books for the coming year.

◆

Boxer shorts with team logos, sayings, or graphics such as smiley faces, hearts, snowmen, or tropical fish. Check out JoeBoxer.com for a wide selection of styles for men and women.

◆

Potted plants or seedlings.

"It's All Fun and Games" Favors and Prizes

Some of your shower games will call for playful prizes and gag gifts. So check out the following items at party supply or toy stores and give your guests a giggle:

❤

Magic 8 ball.

❤

Etch-a-Sketch.

❤

Slinky toys.

❤

Pez dispensers.

❤

Action figure characters (for extra fun, choose ones whose faces bear a resemblance to your guests).

❤

Yo-yos.

❤

Fun sunglasses.

❤

Fuzzy handcuffs.

❤

Water guns.

❤

Glow-in-the-dark stickers for bedroom ceilings.

❤

Lunch boxes.

❤

Cartoon character items.

❤

Mini-puzzles.

❤

Joke books.

♥

Unusual music tapes, such as college fight songs and yodeling.

♥

Mad Libs.

Favor Bars

No, not chocolate bars. These are lineups of craft supplies at a table where guests create their own custommade favors in a scent, color, or design of their choosing. Consider the following:

Massage oil bar. You supply small bottles of oil and a variety of scented essential oils (rose, musk, lemon, sandalwood, and so on). Guests can mix their own scents by combining several favorites for a unique blend.

Bath salt bar. Set out pretty containers of scented and colored bath salts, along with scoops and empty containers in a variety of shapes. Guests create their own layered bath salt dispensers in colors that match their bathroom decor.

Potpourri bar. Set out several different kinds of potpourri mixes, along with several different kinds of containers. Guests can choose their favorites or make a mixture.

◎

PART 3

Now This Is a Party!

Fifty Great Shower Themes

Women - Only Showers

12

Here we go! Check out the following ladies-only theme ideas and details. (Many of the co-ed shower concepts in the next chapter can work for your all-female crowd as well.)

Hawaiian Luau

Description

Take a trip to the Hawaiian Islands without leaving the mainland! Your luau shower will transport guests to a paradise of warm sun and sand, palm trees, and delicious tropical drinks.

Decor

If you can hold the shower outside at sunset, especially near a pool with a fountain, you're in great shape. Light some tiki torches around the grounds, set tropical flower wreaths and candles in the pool, and enjoy the nighttime summer air.

- -

For all of the themes in this chapter and the following chapter, the Web sites below can help you plan the menu, beverages, decor, and favors and individualize your party according to the guest of honor and the guests:

All Posters (for decorating the room, prizes, and favors):
   www.allposters.com

Appetizers.com: www.Appetizers.com

Bookstore sites: (for gift books, CDs, DVDs, and videos):
   www.amazon.com or www.bn.com

Cocktails.com: www.cocktails.com

The Food Network: www.foodtv.com

Illuminations (candles): www.illuminations.com

Recipe Source: www.recipesource.com

Wine Spectator: www.winespectator.com

- -

If inside, use real or plastic palm trees, a variety of tropical flowers (such as birds of paradise and stephanotis) in your centerpieces, set out coconuts and pineapples as decorations, and string up fun fish-themed lights. Include posters of Hawaii, ocean scenes, sunsets, surfers, and hula dancers for some added Hawaiian touches.

Menu
Tropical fruit salad, freshly cut pineapple, lomi lomi salmon, seared ahi with mango sauce, tempura, shrimp dishes, mahi mahi curry, Hawaiian pulled pork, pan

fried tofu with seaweed, banana and papaya breads, and a cake with macadamia nut filling and accents.

Drinks

Serve drinks in tall glasses with slices of fruit or drink umbrellas, or serve them in real or plastic coconut shells.

Go for the tropical concoctions—Blue Hawaii, Mai Tai, Piña Colada—and frozen daiquiris.

Games

"What's Under Your Skirt?" Guests don grass skirts, perhaps to do an impromptu hula dance. Those with a certain color tag on the band of the skirt win a prize.

Use colorful leis for a variation of "The Clothespin Game," in which a certain word is considered taboo for the night. If one guest hears another guest say the word, the hearer takes the speaker's lei and puts it around her own neck.

Favors

Plastic coconuts filled with wrapped candies or chocolates.

Surf's Up key chains.

Conch shells.

Tiny framed seahorses or starfish.

Sunglasses.

Beach bags filled with shore paraphernalia such as sunscreen, sunglasses, a beach-read novel, and a CD of classic Hawaiian music.

A Little Something Extra

Have a few of your hosts learn an authentic hula dance (like the *huki lau*) and then teach the entire group these simple traditional moves.

Do a little research on the Internet to find and print out Hawaiian marriage blessings and prayers, or mystical island legends about weddings and royal marriages.

Play Hawaiian music, like *Sounds of Hawaii*, *Hawaii's Greatest Hits* or *Drew's Famous Hawaiian Luau Party* soundtracks.

English Afternoon Tea

Description

Don't forget to lift your pinkie as you sip your tea! The English afternoon tea can be an elegant gathering in a sitting room, or an outdoor spread right out of Jane Austen's *Emma*.

Decor

If you are outdoors, set up tables under wide umbrellas, or find a shady spot in a field.

◆

If you are indoors, appoint a lovely sitting room with well-dressed tables, including fine china and crystal in different but complementary colors and patterns. Silver platters are a must, as is a collection of elegant tea serving sets.

◆

Purchase heart-shaped sugar cubes.

◆

White and blush-colored flowers make beautiful centerpieces, as do white and blush-colored pillar or votive candles. Attach small floral bunches to the backs of chairs or to napkin rings for an added dose of high society style.

Menu

Tea sandwiches, crudités, smoked salmon, fruit and nut breads, scones and crumpets, mini-quiches, petit fours and pastries, fruit-covered meringue tartlets, and a beautifully decorated circular cake with lacy swirled icing and pastel-colored flowers.

Drinks

Earl Gray tea if you'd like to be authentic, or an array of flavored teas, chai, and green tea.

◆

"Spike" the tea as well, if that's to your crowd's liking; add crème de cacao to a mint tea, Malibu rum to a mango or fruit-flavored tea. Experiment with these frisky mixes ahead of time, and be sure to include coffee and nonalcoholic punch for those party-draggers who don't like tea.

Games
Use little bridal charms attached to thin ribbon lengths and embedded in the icing layer of a cake. Your guests gently pull a ribbon to retrieve their charms. The horseshoe means good luck, the coin means prosperity, and the wedding ring means the bearer will be the next to marry (or enjoy a long and happy marriage). Find these and additional charms at wedding supply Web sites or in catalogs.

Favors
Single flowers wrapped in cellophane and tied with a ribbon.

◆

A single gardenia in a clear plastic box.

◆

Charm bracelets.

◆

A flower-themed gift book.

◆

A book of love poetry or sonnets.

◆

A gift-size cookbook of teas and tea cakes.

◆

Classical music CDs.

◆

Videos or DVDs of movies made from Jane Austen novels (*Emma* and *Sense and Sensibility*) or another favorite British movie.

◆

For tea-lovers, create baskets of flavored teas (see www .rishitea.com, www.leaves.com, or www.truetea.com) or give teapots, honey bear bottles with personalized labels, tea infusers, flavored honeys, or copies of *Teas for All Seasons* by Shelly Richardson and Bruce Richardson.

A Little Something Extra
Read aloud some short poetry from Elizabeth Barrett Browning or Robert Browning.

◆

Play music such as *Classical Dreams: Music to Inspire*.

◆

Ask the ladies to wear their best hats to the affair.

The Italian Countryside

Description
Take to Tuscan hillsides and fig groves, vineyards and castles, with an Italian countryside bridal shower, where food and drink is the central element of the day.

Decor

Transform a backyard into the Tuscan valley by setting up under the shade of an old expansive tree.

❤

Outdoors or in, create an authentic serving table by setting out two big wine barrels and laying a door or wooden tabletop on them. Cover this rustic table with your serving dishes and bowls of grapes, nuts, and flowers in deep purples and burgundies.

❤

Provide plenty of flowers, if not in a border garden then as centerpieces and cuttings. Grape clusters make excellent accents to this shower, as do bowls of figs, nuts, tomatoes, peppers, and fruits.

Menu

Breads and grissini (long, thin breadsticks) with various tapenade spreads and cheese, fruits, roasted red peppers, tomato bruschetta, mixed green salads, and pasta and meat dishes with authentic Italian flavors.

❤

Visit an Italian gourmet store or deli to select some wonderful prosciutto, marinated vegetables, spiced mozzarella balls, goat cheeses, and salamis.

❤

For dessert, choose a rum cake, pizzelles (delicate, lacy fried dough cookies in the shape of stars, and dusted with confectioner's sugar), or fresh berries in a liqueur sauce.

Drinks

Only the finest Italian wines will do. Choose a variety of whites and reds (see www.winespectator.com).

♥

After-dinner drinks might include espresso or cappuccino with Sambuca, with coffee beans and lemon twists floating on top.

Games

Ask your older-generation Italian friends and relatives how to play the games of their youth.

♥

An old Italian group game à la "rock, paper, scissors" has everyone in a circle, but they each hold out one to five fingers while simultaneously shouting out, in Italian, the number they think will be the total of *all* the held-out fingers in the circle. Have each table play as a group, give everyone a printout of how to pronounce the numbers in Italian, and stand back . . . because the outbursts get loud and fun.

Favors

♥

Tomato plant seedlings.

♥

Wine charms.

♥

Postcard books of Italian paintings.

❤

Grape-imprinted coasters.

❤

CDs of Italian music.

❤

Containers of marinated mozzarella balls or pizzelles.

❤

Small, picture-filled cookbooks of Italian appetizers and other recipes.

❤

Bottles of Italian wine or liqueurs.

❤

Bags of chocolate-covered espresso beans.

A Little Something Extra

No trip to the Italian countryside would be complete without Italian opera or classical music in the background. So dust off your collection of classical CDs, or go get the new Andrea Boccelli recording, and serenade your guests with music that will take them "home" to Italy.

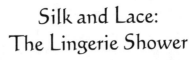

Silk and Lace:
The Lingerie Shower

Description

Shower the bride who has everything with lingerie: silk, lace, thongs, teddies, marabou slippers, and other accoutrements for her saucier side.

Decor

Turn the room into a romantic or sexy boudoir by changing the curtains to a lavish pink or red, and drape boas or silk fabrics on tables and countertops.

Add flickering scented pillar or votive candles, rose petals on the table, and thick floral centerpieces with color-coordinated variations of pink or red blooms.

Menu

Standard buffet party fare or set up several melted-chocolate fondue pots surrounded by cubes of fruit, angel food cake, pound cake, even carrot cake.

Buy or make frosted cookies in the shapes of angels, devils, high-heeled shoes, even bras! Don't forget the chocolate-covered strawberries and apricots, with plenty of fresh whipped cream.

Drinks

Sexy drinks are on call for this party, so serve bright martinis and Cosmopolitans, or go to www.cocktail.com for drinks with racy names.

Games

The racier the better!

Some crowds have a "Fake Orgasm Contest," for which contestants put on their best moaning-in ecstasy-performance, and the rest of the guests vote for the winner.

Play "Name That Movie" and use quotes from sexy movies.

Read humorous Do's and Don'ts advice from party guests on maintaining a hot sex life during marriage.

Favors
Chocolates shaped as high heels.

Handcuffs.

Angels, devils, or roses.

CDs of romantic music.

Gift books on romance, sex, and love, such as *The Kama Sutra*.

Baskets of romantic goodies such as chocolates, massage oils, feathers, and a romantic music CD; sexy-themed movie videos and DVDs or stripping how-to videos; guidebooks on massage for lovers; imprinted panties in a range of sizes; perfumes; massage oil kits.

A Little Something Extra

This is a good party for a performance by a male exotic dancer (or a trio of male dancers). Have him (or them) arrive at the end of the party when everyone's all riled up from faking their orgasms, and when the older and more conservative guests have left.

Under the Sea

Description

Picture the world of *The Little Mermaid*, and then re-create it for an undersea experience.

Decor

Blue walls (if you can do it), bright-colored tropical fish suspended from the ceiling (not real ones, of course), along with strings of clear crystals to create a bubble effect.

◆

In the corners, position some bright-colored beanbag chairs to look like the rocks in a fish tank.

◆

For table centerpieces, use bunches of bright tropical fish balloons or even a fishbowl with live goldfish, surrounded by seashells and sand sprinkled on the tablecloth.

◆

Make an anchor out of Styrofoam and aluminum foil and set it against the wall, along with a sunken treasure chest filled with shiny fake jewels and old coins.

◆

Set out some plastic lobsters and crabs from the craft store, and hang from the ceiling lengths of fishing wire with big, fake, aluminum foil fishing hooks attached.

◆

All of your plates and glasses can be tropical-fish imprinted, or pearlized blue to look as though they came from the bottom of the sea.

Menu
Seafood bites such as shrimp cocktail, stuffed clams, fried calamari, bacon-wrapped scallops, king crab legs, salads, and pastas with clam sauce.

◆

Shape your cake like a clamshell, and decorate it with sea characters for flair.

Drinks
Serve bright blue martinis and give them an undersea name, like Neptune's Nectar, or go to www.cocktail.com to find out how to make a Barracuda Bite, a Sea Horse, a Reef Runner, or a Tidal Wave.

◆

Pop a starfish-topped drink stirrer or some Gummi-candy fish into each glass for sweet flavoring.

Games
Set a small plastic treasure chest in front of each place setting. Fill each treasure chest with wrapped candies and chocolate raspberry-filled starfish from Godiva. The one treasure chest that also holds a mermaid doll (or starfish, seahorse, or little rubber shark) wins a prize.

◆

Have guests write down or sing songs that contain ocean themes or certain words (sea, ocean, beach, shark, or others).

Favors
Starfish charms or key chains.

◆

Framed seashell prints.

◆

Ocean-theme printed candles and votive holders.

◆

Ocean-themed calendars, notepads, magnets, or postcards.

◆

Guests can also take home the live goldfish centerpieces.

A Little Something Extra
For your party's ambience, create CD mixes that contain music with a sea theme. They could be musical scores complete with whale songs or the soundtrack from Disney's *The Little Mermaid*.

Fairy Tales Come True

Description
We all want to believe in fairy tales, right? Forget the real world for a few hours and welcome your guests to a

fairy-tale land complete with castles, dragons, and sprite-like creatures from the woods.

Decor

If you can't book your party at a castle or estate home that looks like a castle, you can turn the party room into a scene right out of a fairy tale.

❤

Decorate a set of chairs as thrones, set out a red carpet leading to them, and fill a corner of the room with rented potted trees for an enchanted forest.

❤

Set out signs with messages from your favorite fairy tales, such as "Beware of Big Bad Wolf" next to the wooded entrance to your home or a "Do Not Eat" sign next to a ripe red apple in a glass case (it was Snow White's downfall, after all).

❤

Centerpieces can be elaborately jeweled crowns (bought or homemade by the kids), glass slippers on red velvet pillows, open bags of magic beans (coffee beans bought in bulk, which also give the room a nice scent), pump-kins (which you replace during the games with home-made royal carriages), or floral centerpieces containing magic wands.

❤

Hang a big mirror on the wall and instruct guests to ask it their deepest question. Keep a stack of the mirror's "responses," which you have printed beforehand on cards, in a nearby holder for guests to draw their response as delivered by the all-knowing mirror. Or go higher tech by pre-recording a series of fun answers on a tape recorder for guests to push the play button after each asking.

Menu

A lavish buffet with butter, creams, and sauces served in plastic "glass" slippers. Add in "magic beans" as a side dish, pumpkin bread, gingerbread cookies.

💜

Provide a sheet cake decorated with the bride's favorite fairy-tale character, and surround the cake with Hershey's Kisses (Get it—true love's first kiss?).

Drinks

Brightly colored martinis.

💜

Frozen margaritas (you can call them Snow White's Kisses).

💜

Flavored coffees to keep your guests from turning into Sleeping Beauties.

Games

Twist those fairy tales. Each table of guests gets a card with the beginning of a well-known fairy tale written on it. They then have to compose a modernized version of the story and read it aloud. How fun that Cinderella sued her evil stepmother for emotional and physical abuse, won $25 million dollars, and bought a condo for her Fairy Godmother in Palm Springs!

Favors

Copies of the *Into the Woods* soundtrack.

❤

Ever After or other video or DVD.

❤

Magic wands.

❤

Bubble makers.

❤

Chocolates.

❤

Star ornaments to wish upon.

❤

Fairy-tale books.

❤

Cinderella collectibles.

❤

Photo albums for when dreams do come true.

A Little Something Extra

If the groom is a very good sport (make that a candidate for sainthood), he might agree to dress up like a knight in shining armor or the bride's Prince Charming for that one true love's kiss before he has to go catch the game at the sports bar with his buddies.

❤

Rent a Princess costume for the bride to change into for the duration of her party.

Dress up little girl guests as fairies, complete with fairy wings and magic wands.

Back to Your Roots

Description
Whatever the bride's ethnic background, build the shower as an inclusive tribute to her heritage and family.

Decor
Choose decor that fits with the heritage theme, such as a pagoda for a Japanese party, an Oktoberfest for a German theme. Visit party supply or even ethnic-based stores and Web sites for supplies and ideas.

For wall art, go to www.allposters.com to find prints and posters that work with the selected region.

Menu
Choose a menu that fits with the ethnic flavor. Go to www.foodtv.com, www.recipesearch.com, or to individual ethnic centers' Web sites for recipes and suggestions, or to ethnic markets.

Drinks
Choose a drink that works with the theme, such as French wines and liqueurs for a French party, an array of vodkas for your Ukrainian friend's party, or various drinks listed at www.cocktail.com according to regions.

Games

Do a little research to find games that fit with the ethnic theme. Talk to family elders to find out what games they played back in the old country.

Print cards with words written in the region's language, and let everyone guess their meanings.

Favors

Check ethnic-based Web sites for ideas, or go to www .amazon.com or www.bn.com for gift books, graphic books, music, or movies that fit with your theme.

A Little Something Extra

Have a relative or friend who is fluent in the language and culture of that nationality create cards with translations of each guest's first and last names.

Have a family elder prepare a little speech about the bride's family origins in "the old country" and how and when they came to America.

International Night

Description

Bring the world to the bride's feet with a collection of culture and flavors from around the globe.

Decor

Have each table represent a different country, complete with the flag of that country, perhaps dolls in regional dress, and other items from the culture (such as wooden shoes from the Netherlands or marriage ducks from Korea).

◆

Hang or display travel prints or posters from each country around the room, and include flowers from each country as well (tulips, of course, from the Netherlands, African violets, poppies from the Middle East).

Menu
At the buffet table or at each table, serve and label a dish from each country, making your menu a veritable United Nations.

◆

Serve a plain sheet cake that displays flags from all the nations you've included in your festivities.

Drinks
Go global again, with wines, beers, and liquors from various countries (see www.winespectator.com).

Games
For "Name That Flag," guests guess which flag belongs to which country.

◆

Translate a saying, such as "Best wishes on your marriage," into other languages, and have guests guess the languages.

Favors
International music CDs.

◆

Gift books of travel photos from each country.

◆

Wine bottles.

◆

International brand candies (such as Toblerone).

A Little Something Extra
Plan a performance for the party. You might bring in a troupe of Irish dancers, a pair of ballet dancers, a yodeler, whatever might make your party an international experience. Have hosts or guests volunteer to perform, which can be funny as well as fun.

The Haunted Shower

Description
Great for Halloween-time showers, this spooky soirée revolves around horror movies or the supernatural.

Decor
Set out some fake tombstones on your front lawn or in a corner of the party room, and use fun Halloween decorations from the party store.

♥

Buy fake plastic eyeballs and float them in the punch.

♥

Center each of your tables with an Ouija board, a tall black witch's hat, a cross and some garlic, or a hockey mask or other notable item from horror movies.

♥

Give each table a horror movie theme if you wish, or just go with the ghost motif, draping each chair with a white sheet painted with a ghost face.

❤

Rent a dry ice machine and use it to fill the room with an eerie mist, and creatively arrange fake cobwebs on banisters, mantels, tables, and in corners.

Menu
General buffet fare, touched with a bit of the spooky stuff: a rice and noodle salad can be called a worm and maggot stew, and anything with a red sauce poured over the top is *Carrie*-esque.

Drinks
Zombies are a great idea for your hard-drinking crowd, but any colorful mixed drink or punch can be "scarified" by dropping in those plastic eyeballs or Gummi worms.

❤

Try out the Demon Possession, Skeleton, and Cannibal drinks at www.cocktail.com.

Games
Tell a great ghost story, of course, or do a progressive telling where a guest gives one sentence of a ghost tale and the others add onto it in turn. For a little help, check out ghost-story books in the library or a bookstore.

Favors
Chocolate-molded candies and cutout/frosted cookies in the shapes of spiders, ghosts, or howling werewolves.

❤

Videos and DVDs of classic horror movies.

❤

Collections of Edgar Allan Poe's short stories and poetry.

❤

Audiobooks of Vincent Price reading Edgar Allen Poe's *The Raven* or *The Telltale Heart*.

❤

My favorite: a guidebook on local haunted houses with a tour map and mini-flashlight.

A Little Something Extra
Play spooky music in the background, such as the CDs *Ultimate Halloween Party*, *Halloween Howls*, *Fright Night*, and *Halloween Big Screen Thrillers*.

❤

Use a taped werewolf's howl during the games as the guest prize signifier.

❤

Have all guests come in costumes.

❤

"'Rig" the party space to have ghostlike movements occur (such as doors swinging open or lights flickering).

Broadway

Description
Come and meet those dancing feet at a Broadway bridal shower.

Decor

Hang posters of the biggest shows on the Great White Way: *42nd Street*, *Into the Woods*, *Phantom of the Opera*, *Rent*, and so on.

Have each table represent a smash hit Broadway play or musical and decorate accordingly; for instance, put a black hat and that creepy white phantom's mask on the *Phantom of the Opera* table, or a pile of stuffed, fluffy kitties on the *Cats* table.

Create invitations, table menus, and place cards in the design of playbills.

Use dramatic spotlights to make your party world a stage.

Menu

Go elegant with a lavish buffet à la the menu at Sardi's—caviar-filled endive, mesclun salad, lobster tails, bananas flambé—and serve all courses with dramatic flair.

Drinks

Champagne, elegant cocktails. Nothing's too good for the toast of the town.

Games

Play "Name That Tune;" guests have to match the belted-out Broadway song to the musical it came from.

Play "Match That Star;" guests are given a list of celebrities and they have to name the Broadway show each starred in.

Try out "Write the Sequel;" each table of guests comes up with the story line for the sequel to a well-known play (as in *Cats 2: All the Cats Move to the Suburbs Where They are Spayed and Neutered and Given Boring Names Like "Fluffy"*).

Favors
Original cast recordings of Broadway plays.
Inexpensive tickets to local community theater renditions of musicals or dramas.

Toy microphones for belting out those torch songs.

T-shirts printed with a play's title.

Chocolate-molded Tony awards.

Shiny foil-wrapped chocolate stars.

A Little Something Extra
Recruit hosts to dress up like the Rockettes in stockings, glittery leotards, and sparkling hats for a welcoming kick-line when the bride arrives.

Buy toy trophies and give out Tony awards to guests for fun categories: Best Performance during the games or Best Costume Design for her daring purple dangle earrings and matching scarf.

Seat the bride in a director's chair with her name emblazoned on it, or dress her up like a backstage Broadway diva in a white silk robe and boa.

In the Kitchen

Description
Stock up the bride's kitchen with gourmet goodies, gadgets, and . . . oh, yeah, a blender.

Decor
Standard party decor. Just pick a color theme for centerpieces and linens.

Menu
Choose a variety of great buffet food selections, from appetizers to entrées to desserts (see chapter 6 for ideas).

The key is the presentation, setting menu items on platters and decorating with sprigs of mint and swirls of sauces, just like you see in those gourmet food magazines.

Drinks
Serve the Kitchen Wall, a butterscotch schnapps and Bailey's coffee mixture, or other appropriate cocktail (see www.cocktail.com).

◆

A simple punch and soft drinks.

◆

Warm and cozy teas and coffees.

Games

Collect unusual kitchen gadgets and have guests make up a fun and funky not-true alternate use for them (such as "This rolling pin can also be used to massage your husband's back").

◆

Add some spice to the bride's future marriage by having guests pull cooking spice bottles from a bag and say what each spice represents for the bride (for instance, "Thyme—may you and your groom enjoy countless happy times together," "Sage—may you both always have access to the sage wisdom of your family and long-married couples with joyous marriages," or "Chili powder—may you have the hottest, spiciest sex life!").

Favors

Flavored olive oils.

◆

Potted herb plants.

◆

Baskets of flavored sauces and gourmet goodies.

◆

Theme-printed potholders or spoon rests.

◆

A kitschy egg timer.

◆

Cookbooks and small gift recipe books.

◆

Packets of vegetable seeds for the planting of a bountiful kitchen garden.

◆

Bulk-buy the books *Goddess in the Kitchen* by Margie Lapanja and *Wild Women in the Kitchen: 101 Rambunctious Recipes and 99 Tasty Tales* by Nicole Alper, Lynette Rohrer, and the Wild Women Association. This latter one is a collection of recipes from and stories about famous women in history and the arts, such as Elizabeth Taylor, Lucille Ball, Eleanor Roosevelt, and Cleopatra, to name a few).

A Little Something Extra
Have guests make some of the dishes or desserts you serve and ask them to bring copies of their recipes on colored paper or index cards for the bride and all the guests (give them the head count beforehand so they know how many copies to bring).

Pick a Room, Any Room

Description
Get out of the kitchen and into the bedroom, living room, or especially the bride's home office. The room-specific bridal shower helps the couple create a fully

stocked specialty room in their house as guests bring them everything they need to decorate, say, a luxurious bedroom or spa-worthy bathroom.

Decor
Use standard color-coordinated decorations with theme-appropriate accents in centerpieces.

❤

For a bedroom shower, move a beautiful twin bed into a corner of the party room (complete with matching linens, pretty stuffed pillows, and duvet cover) and use that to hold the guests' gifts.

Menu
Standard menu fare (see chapter 6 for ideas), with room-appropriate items as well.

❤

Try a dessert buffet of "foods you'd eat in bed:" ice cream, cookies, chocolate cake.

Drinks
Choose from the standards: wine, cocktails, soft drinks, coffee, and tea.

❤

Name any cocktails after the room in question, such as Bedroom Eyes Bourbon and Coke, Home Office Hurricane, or Sunroom Sangria.

Games
Use several different-colored pillowcases (look for satin, leopard-striped, and children's designs to make it fun!) and put an unusual item from the bedroom in each,

such as an alarm clock or a candleholder. Have guests try to guess what each item is only by feeling it through the pillowcase fabric.

❤

For a home office shower (which is *very* popular right now), put various desk items from an office supply store into a plastic bag and have the guests try to guess what each item is by feeling it through the bag.

Favors
Bedroom:

> Satin pillowcases
>
> Fuzzy slippers
>
> A collection of bedtime books to read, such as novels or even the book *Bedroom Feng Shui* by Clear Englebert

❤

Home office:

> Brightly colored bunches of pencils (I love the smiley-face and hologram ones from the craft store!)
>
> Business card holders
>
> Design-printed computer mouse pads

❤

Entertainment room:

> Guests choose from a selection of CDs, DVDs and movie videos.

A Little Something Extra
For a home office shower, present the bride with an elegant engraved name plate for her desk or office door.

For a bedroom shower's background sound, play classical romantic music, such as the CDs sold in Victoria's Secret stores and at www.victoriassecret.com.

Lap of Luxury

Description
It's all pampering all the time at this spa-inspired party.

Decor
The trickling drops of a portable water fountain (or several) create a relaxing sound.

Use soft pastel colors in linens and floral centerpieces.

Votive candles and pastel or white pillar candles of various heights, encircled with scattered rose petals, can also serve as centerpieces.

Be sure the room is aromatic by lighting scented candles early and stocking it with the most fragrant flowers: gardenias and stargazer lilies.

Use flowing linens and drapes to add a softened look to the room.

Menu
Delicious spa fare, such as poached salmon with wonderfully seasoned vegetables, veggie quiche, mixed-greens

salads with incredible and unusual salad dressings (see www.foodtv.com for recipes such as mango and dill-flavored dressings), fruit-topped Chantilly-cream tartlets, and a frosted and fruit-covered sheet cake with chocolate-dipped strawberries and truffles on the side (Chocolate is, after all, great for your brain and calming to the soul!).

Drinks
Mimosas, champagne, and brightly colored cocktails.

Fruit smoothies (for luscious recipes, check out the book *Ultimate Smoothies* by Donna Rodnitzky).

Green tea and flavored coffees.

Ice water with slices of lemon, lime, and orange, and cherries.

Games
Prizes go to the guest who can sniff out and accurately identify the scents of essential oils in numbered but un-labeled bottles. Have them write down their guesses. You can get little oil bottles at aromatherapy centers or stores such as The Body Shop.

Winners of any game you play get a gift certificate for a massage, hot rock therapy, paraffin treatment, or other indulgence at a spa near them.

Favors
Aromatherapy products.

※

Votive candles and holders.

※

Gift books on stress-relief and self-care advice such as Sark's *Eat Mangoes Naked* or Jennifer Louden's *Couples Comfort Book.*

※

Relaxing music CDs such as R. Carlos Nakai's Native American music (find the collection on www.amazon .com or www.bn.com).

※

Plush robes and slippers.

※

Eye masks.

※

Baskets of luxuriant lotion and cream sample bottles.

※

Lip gloss collections—see the pampering products Web sites listed in Resources (page 293).

A Little Something Extra
Hire a masseur or foot massage therapist to give your guests a blissful, professional rubdown.

※

As an extra activity, stock a make-your-own bar of massage lotions, scented oils, or custom perfumes for guests to make their own concoctions.

Flower Shower

Description

Everything's coming up roses (or lilies or tulips) at your flower-themed shower.

Decor

Set your tables with pastel, rose and pink tablecloths and a gorgeous array of elegant and unique flowers as a centerpiece on each.

Use floral-printed dishes and glasses, napkins, and even chair covers. Put candles at each place setting to complete the look.

Set potted trees and flowering bushes in the corners of the room, with smaller potted plants on mantels and windowsills.

Bring an outdoor garden bench or outdoor swing inside, along with a wheelbarrow filled with potted flowers.

Menu

Standard menu fare, with thoughtful floral presentations such as edible flower petals (see chapter 6) sprinkled over an entrée or dessert, long-stemmed roses laid in arranged bunches directly on the buffet table, daisy designs piped onto the cake, cupcakes, or petit fours, and flower-shaped and brightly frosted sugar cookies.

Drinks

Colorful flower-hued mixed drinks or punches sprinkled with edible flower petals, wines, and champagne.

◆

Give each drink a flower-power name, such as Daffodil Daiquiri or Peony Punch.

◆

Freeze mini-blooms of edible flowers into ice cubes, or buy flower-shaped plastic ice cubes to freeze and reuse.

Games
Set out pictures of exotic flowers and have guests fill out game cards to name each bloom. The easy ones are obvious: tulip, rose, bird of paradise. But when you get to peonies versus ranunculus, there's bound to be a challenge.

◆

Do a blindfolded scent test, where guests are asked to identify each flower by aroma.

◆

Have guests ask a question such as, "Will we close on the house this month?" or "Is my blind date this weekend going to be a success?" and then pick each petal off a daisy in a he-loves-me/he-loves-me-not style to arrive at the answer.

Favors
Flower-printed gift items like candles and candleholders.

◆

Flower notepads.

◆

Flower magnets.

Coffee mugs printed with flowers.

Framed pictures featuring flowers.

Packs of flower postcards.

Garden-themed calendars.

Flower-shaped key chains.

Floral scent perfumes (such as Sunflowers), or rose- or gardenia-scented hand lotions or room sprays.

◆

Cute gardening gloves, baskets of flower seeds, and a mini-trowel for the green thumbs on your guest list.

◆

Purchase pretty petal gift boxes for perfect (and easy) wrapping for your gifts (see www.bayleysboxes.com).

A Little Something Extra

Find out the bride's favorite flower and build your shower around that. Also, talk to the bride's mother, grandmother, and future mother-in-law for *their* favorite blooms to incorporate into the day. Make a special presentation about the bride's departed grandmother's love of gardenias or the mom's prize-winning violets to add a sentimental touch to the day.

Favorite Entertainer

Description

For the bride who has everything . . . except that one dream meeting with her favorite entertainer. For the sake of brevity—and because I'm hoping that Sting will read this when his daughter gets married and be so impressed that he'll pick me up for dinner in a limo (with his wife, Trudie, of course)—let's use Sting as the example.

Decor

A variety of posters of Sting (see www.allposters.com) strategically placed on easels or mantels.

❤

Centerpieces might include a displayed album cover or CD surrounded by candles and set on top of sheet music (find those at bookstores or photocopy a library's collection on colored or off-white paper).

❤

Have televisions around the room running videotapes or DVDs of Sting in performance, with the sound of only one turned up enough to provide background music.

Menu

Standard menu fare, but perhaps studded with tiny bee toys, chocolate-covered yellow and black bees, and bees on toothpicks and drink stirrers.

Drinks
Of course, it would be the Stinger (see www.cocktail
.com), or any variety of standard party drinks or punches.

Games
Read a line from a Sting song, and guests have to
"Name That Tune."

♥

Set out poster board with the name of each Sting song
on it, and guests have to record their favorite memory
that arises whenever they hear that song.

♥

Guests have to guess how many times the bride has
seen Sting in concert.

Favors
Sting and Police CDs.

♥

Photo albums.

♥

Stationery and fine pen sets (for writing fan letters!)

♥

Gift certificates to a music store for guests to buy their
own favorites' new releases.

♥

Since Sting is a yoga fanatic, favors might include a
yoga videotape, music to do yoga by, or how-to books on

One of the most popular Favorite Entertainer showers for women is the Audrey Hepburn shower. Have your guests dress like Holly Golightly in a simple black sheath dress, pearls, and sunglasses, with upswept hair. Run videos or display posters from Ms. Hepburn's classic movies (see www.allposters.com for a wealth of posters, from Breakfast at Tiffany's, My Fair Lady, and Charade to glamour shots of the star).

the art and practice of yoga. (Check www.yogazone.com for additional ideas, such as the Om pendant.)

A Little Something Extra

Surprise the bride with two tickets to see her favorite entertainer in person when his or her tour comes to town. Arrange ahead of time with the groom to see if he wants to jump in here and book a hotel suite in the city to make the night extra special.

Heart of Gold

Description

The bride works hard for her favorite charity, and you can support her heart of gold by forming the shower around her cause.

NOTE: For some Heart of Gold showers, hosts and guests skip the party and plan instead for everyone on the guest list to participate in a breast cancer walk (either as a walker or a volunteer along the way) or spend a weekend working on a Habitat for Humanity house, for instance.

Decor

Choose a decor theme that works with the charity in question, as in big red hearts for her work with a heart foundation.

Menu

Standard party fare, with those theme-appropriate icons worked into the food, desserts, and presentation of all courses. For instance, cut finger sandwiches into heart shapes with a cookie cutter, or make heart-shaped petit fours.

Drinks

Choose from wines, punches, and cocktails, giving each libation an appropriate name, such as Panda Punch for the World Wildlife Federation lover, or Save the Baby Seals Chardonnay.

Games

It's never appropriate to ask guests for money, so don't even think about playing games for cash and then donating to the cause, or holding an auction at a shower. Look at the games in chapter 8 to see how you can tweak them to fit a charity theme.

Place a sealed box containing a chocolate heart in front of each place setting, and ask guests to open them at a designated time. The guest who gets the chocolate wrapped in gold foil—the Heart of Gold—wins the prize.

Favors

Items bought from the charity's Web site, such as the timber wolf or panda note cards, magnets, and mugs from the World Wildlife Federation, pink heart ribbon pins from a breast cancer site, and so on.

A Little Something Extra

You and the other hosts can announce that you've made a sizeable donation to the bride's favorite charity in her name.

Secretly obtain a thank-you note from a woman the bride has helped at the battered women's shelter or retirement home. (NOTE: request this from the shelter or home's coordinator to afford the recipient her anonymity.) Reading it at the shower is likely to bring tears to the bride's eyes.

Holistic Shower

Description

Find inner peace with a feng-shui designed holistic bridal shower.

Decor

Make it as calm an environment as the Lap of Luxury party on page 204, but add in the trademark props of the holistic life: grounding earth tones, crystals, and feng shui accoutrements such as wind chimes.

Menu

Spa cuisine works well, as does Japanese cuisine or Middle Eastern fare, and cookies piped with good luck symbols or mandalas.

Drinks

Green tea, brightly colored cocktails, even champagne to symbolize the richness of life.

Games

For the tapping of insightful inner wisdom, use the *Contemplation Cards* deck by Susan Woldman (www.susanwoldman.com). Have the guest pose a question to the universe about some matter in her life, then pull three cards from the deck to represent the current situation, what to do about it, and what the outcome will be. She or someone else can read the answers.

Favors

Feng-shui workbooks or card decks.

◆

Yoga card decks.

◆

Wind chimes (www.pyramidcollection.com).

◆

Stones imprinted with inspirational words or symbols for your garden or home.

◆

Essential oils.

◆

Mandala note cards (www.mandalaconnections.com).

◆

Flower vases and seedlings.

◆

Candles and votive holders.

◆

Good luck feng-shui charms such as those for travel, money, love, luck, and career success (www.mjgdesigns .com).

A Little Something Extra

Have a tarot card reader on hand to tell people their futures and fortunes; hire a professional or enlist the help of an experienced mystical friend.

Fly Me to the Moon

Description

Stargazers will love this trip to the moon as a starry, starry night becomes the setting for your bridal shower.

Decor

Generously decorate the room with shiny stars on the walls and hanging from the ceiling. Include constellations in gold colors to make them stand out, shooting stars, a big half moon, and even a suspended toy of the space shuttle for perspective.

Centerpieces might include moon rocks, painted Styrofoam moons or stars, or even little alien creature toys for a kick.

Menu

Standard menu fare, with items cut with a cookie cutter into star and moon shapes.

Add Moon Pies to the dessert table spread for fun.

Don't forget to provide proof that the moon *is* made out of cheese by carving a block of gouda or cheddar into a moon shape.

Drinks

In addition to the usuals, you've gotta have some Tang!

❤

Name cocktails after astronauts, constellations, and planets.

❤

Buy star-shaped ice cube trays to make theme-appropriate drink-chillers, and purchase star-themed drink stirrers from a party supply or museum store.

Games

Have guests name or sing songs that include the words "moon" or "star(s)," or the names of planets.

❤

Set up a telescope by a window at night to allow guests to gaze at the heavens. Provide a printout of which constellations are currently visible in your night sky, so everyone can find them.

Favors

Star- and moon-shaped chocolates and gift items such as key chains, necklaces, and charm bracelets.

❤

Custom CDs with music such as Tony Bennett's "Fly Me to the Moon" and Elton John's "Rocket Man."

❤

Visit a museum shop to search through their astronomy-inspired gift items and toys.

A Little Something Extra
Name a star after the bride at one of those astronomy Web sites where you can claim your own heavenly body.

Diva Party

Description
Is the bride known as a diva? If so, then throw her a fabulous party where everyone comes as their favorite diva: it might be Mariah, Whitney, Patti, or Cher. Or the bride herself! Everyone dresses and acts in character as their favorite red-hot diva for a stylin' good time. Just keep the big hair away from open flames.

Decor
Throw red fabric over couches and use as curtains, tablecloths, and chair covers for the ultimate spoiled princess dressing-room look. (All white is another option, but that can be drab.)

Stock your room with the kinds of diva requests that celebrities make: plenty of Evian water (chilled) in crystal stemware, bowls of M&Ms with the brown ones picked out, and plenty, plenty, plenty of flowers.

Tack fan letters to the walls, and blow up a glamorous picture of the bride as her "press shot." Some moneyed hosts even create a faux magazine cover with a picture of the bride in a slinky black dress under a celebrity-appropriate headline.

Menu

Make it extravagant—or make it look extravagant. Seafood, caviar-topped appetizers, small lobster tails and grilled shrimp, filet mignon rounds, and a tall, extravagant cake befitting a diva who does everything in a big way.

Drinks

Champagne cocktails, Cosmopolitans, Ruby Reds, wines, and designer waters.

Games

Stand up all the Cher wanna-bes and have the crowd cheer for the best likeness.

Give guests game cards on which they are to write their "diva demands:" those picky, specific, and high-and-mighty requests for the items they want stocked in their dressing rooms. Use a team of judges to choose the most diva-like and give her a certificate for a pampering afternoon at a day spa or a bottle of champagne to take home.

Favors

Handheld mirrors.

CDs of a wide range of divas.

Godiva chocolates.

A diva-saying magnet or bracelet packed in a Tiffany-like light blue box.

A diva-saying bumper sticker.

A Little Something Extra
Videotape each guest's entrance as her favorite diva. With a well-planned custom-made CD, the DJ can play a snippet of a Cher, Mariah, or Madonna track to accompany each guest throwing open the red velvet curtains and stepping into the party room to greet her crowd. Same goes for the bride.

"This Is Your Life"

Description
The bride is regaled with stories from throughout her life, including live and in-person "cameo" appearances from longtime friends and others who "knew her when."

Decor
Decorate the room with pictures of the bride from years past to now—from infancy right up to the present. The more embarrassing (as in those awful clothes and haircuts from a fashion-backwards decade) the better!

Menu
All the bride's favorite foods, set out in marked sections for the decades of her life. Include menu items with a history, such as the chicken salad sandwiches she craved during her college final exams. (One shower group had a friend who still lived near the college go and pick up one of those same sandwiches for authenticity. The bride actually cried!)

Drinks

Serve the bride's favorite drinks. Only her closest friends need to know that the orange juice and peach schnapps drink you're serving is what fueled her first intimate evening with her fiancé.

Games

As host, create an oversize memory book that contains the text to introduce the "characters" from throughout the bride's life. Each character will speak from behind a curtain, telling great tales from the bride's life until she guesses who it is. As an added surprise, help to fly in her long-distance college roommates and childhood best friends and neighbors. One group of hosts invited the bride's fifth-grade science teacher who started her on the road to her current career!

Favors

Journals and photo books with throwaway cameras to record memories.

◆

Postcards and pens to encourage others to get in touch with their faraway loved ones; pre-paid phone cards for the same reason.

A Little Something Extra

Prepare an edited videotape of footage from the bride's life (her first steps, her first day of school, her dancing school days, right up through the present). Add a great handpicked song soundtrack to this home movie reel. Keep it short—10 minutes at the most—as guests get bored easily. Plus, less is more and shorter is sweeter. A skilled editor friend or amateur desktop filmmaker can help you with this task for free.

Royal Treatment

Description

The bride will certainly feel like a princess on her wedding day, so why not get her prepared for the title by throwing a royalty-inspired bridal shower where *everyone* is the queen or princess of something?

Decor

Create a royal castle with the help of some Cinderella-esque props purchased at a party supply store or rented from a costume shop. We're talking a full throne, a red carpet with rose petals sprinkled on it, gold-rimmed dishware, elaborate silverware, and crystal stemware.

You can make enormous royal crests out of oaktag and hang them on the walls; drape brocade fabric to accent curtains, windows, and stairways; and place tall floral centerpieces along with candles on each table.

Use a computer to create fake, colored $100 bills with the bride's picture in the center as her royal currency, and put a few at each place setting.

In a glass display case off to the side, show the Royal Jewels (giant fake gemstone necklaces and earrings).

Menu
An elaborate royal feast or bite-sized delectable appetizers fit for a queen (check www.appetizers.com for ideas).

♥

Choose or make a castle-shaped cake, and supply a royal scepter for cutting it.

Drinks
Champagne, wine, and cocktails named after famous royalty (as in Diana's Diamond Daiquiri and Prince Charles' Sour Apple Martini).

Games
Give each guest a sash on which you've written their royal title. For instance, the bride's sister can be "Sarah, Duchess of Bloomingdale's," and her grandmother can be "The Queen Mum." Have some fun with the names, personalize them, and give guests the option of making their own sashes if they don't like their pre-chosen name. At game-time, each queen, princess, or duchess takes the royal scepter and bestows a new title on the bride (as in "Queen of Good Hair Days").

Favors
Mugs and gift items printed with any variation on the words "queen" and "princess."

♥

Chocolate molded tiaras.

♥

Books about royal family members.

❤

Video or DVD of *The Princess Bride* or *Royal Wedding*.

A Little Something Extra
This won't cost much—contact a local high school or college and pay to have their trumpet soloists come in full uniform to play a quick trumpet call when each guest arrives, and a longer, more pronounced royal horn tribute when the bride arrives to have a royal ball.

Back to the Prom

Description
Get out those poufy, frou-frou prom dresses for another spin around the dance floor. It's a return to the Prom, and a chance to do it all over again without a drunk, sloppy date.

Decor
The cheesier the better. Streamers and balloons are a must, as are oversize banners and theme items hanging from the ceiling. One group of prom-throwers rented one of those disco balls to fill the room with an authentic old-time prom lighting.

Menu
Make it better than that dry chicken you had at your real prom. Choose from the standards in chapter 6, and throw in a few party favorites.

Drinks
Spiked punch, of course.

Games

For "Worst Prom Date," guests tell their prom night-mare stories, such as the date who vomited on her shoes in the limo, the date who disappeared halfway through the night, and the teacher who danced just a little too close for comfort. The guests choose the winner by ballot or applause, finally earning her *something* for that awful prom memory!

Have two or three guests campaign for Prom Queen throughout the evening, with a vote at the end of the party to award the crown (inform the candidates ahead of time so they can bring baskets of homebaked chocolate chip cookies and other fun "bribes" for the voting pool).

Favors

Forget the inscribed wine glasses—no one uses them. Go for items with class (get it?): silver frames, small Godiva chocolate ballotins, candles, CDs.

A Little Something Extra

Play great dance music and have everyone get on the dance floor for line dances, and even spotlight strolls like in the old days.

Back to the '70s/'80s

Description

Break out your '70s fashion ensemble (wait, that stuff's back in now, isn't it?) or '80s *Like a Virgin* look for a time-traveling bridal shower.

Decor

The era-matching outfits you'll tell your guests to wear will provide most of the decor.

◆

Hang posters of '70s and '80s music icons and movies we all remember, and set kitschy culture classics on each table. Add in a table of pictures of the bride and groom from back in the '70s and '80s and you're all set.

Menu

Standard party fare, accented with theme-appropriate goodies you can find at a party supply store.

Drinks

Brightly colored drinks (theme-chosen from www.cocktail.com) and a range of beer and wines.

Games

Say a line from a '70s or '80s era movie, and have players name that movie.

◆

Play a snippet from a popular '70s or '80s song and have guests sing the next few bars of the song or name the singer.

◆

Get out your best accessories and dress up the bride in '80s style (lace stockings, silver crosses, leg warmers, and any other stereotypical fashion statement from that era). Then take plenty of pictures and keep the negatives in a safe place!

Favors

CDs of music from the '70s or '80s, or CDs of popular singers from that era.

Videos or DVDs of Brat Pack movies.

Trivia books or packs of cards focusing on the time period.

BMW key chains.

A Little Something Extra

See if your guests can remember the dance styles of the '70s and '80s. A wide range of age levels love this, since younger guests know the dances, and slightly older guests remember them well. *Footloose, Flashdance, Pretty in Pink*—they all have signature dance moves that are fondly remembered.

Pajama Party

Description

Get the girls together for a good old-fashioned overnight slumber party! The ladies wear their comfiest pajamas, bring along a pillow, sleeping bag, and maybe a teddy bear, and prepare to have their bras thrown in the freezer.

Decor

Use a teenager's or girl's bedroom for this (if someone is generous enough to let you, or away at camp and none the wiser!).

Plenty of posters, pink ruffles, and even a Princess phone for crank calls complete the scene.

Lay out those colorful sleeping bags (have guests borrow their kids' Powerpuff Girls slumber bags!) and the room is ready.

Menu
Pizza, chips, cookies, and a lineup of Ben and Jerry's ice cream flavors, with chocolate and raspberry sauces, sprinkles, and whipped cream for a make-it-yourself sundae bar.

Drinks
Ice cream floats, spiked hot chocolate, wine, or soda.

Games
Tell ghost stories with a wedding themed twist (like the infamous bloody Hook story, only it's hanging off the limo door), watch horror movies, or gossip like mad; make crank calls to a harmless known-to-you recipient or to a faraway friend who couldn't join in the fun.

Play board games, dance till the wee hours, open those shower gifts, and act blissfully silly.

Don't forget to freeze someone's bra or put toothpaste on a guest's hand and tickle her face with a feather. Playing and laughter keeps you young at heart.

Favors
Stuffed animals.

♥

Temporary tattoos.

♥

Travel board games.

♥

Fuzzy slippers.

♥

Gift certificates for free scoops and sundaes at the local ice cream parlor.

A Little Something Extra
What fun would a pajama party be without the boys stopping by in the middle of the night and tossing pebbles at the window? If you want the guys to make an appearance, let them know a good time to cruise by.

Parisian Café

Description
Springtime in Paris . . . strolling along the Champs Élysées . . . dining at an outdoor café . . . taking in the masterpieces at the Louvres. It's all part of the bride's dream trip to Paris, so "take" her there for her bridal shower. Your group of hosts can wear red-and-white striped shirts, slim black Capri pants, and berets, along with a spritz of fine French perfume.

Decor

Set up travel posters of Paris, including the largest shot of the Eiffel Tower you can find.

Set tables with red-and-white checkered tablecloths, baskets of fresh bread, and bottles of wine.

Display copies of artful masterpieces (such as Monets found at www.allposters.com or even prints pulled from your friends' walls!), and surround the scene with potted red-bloom flowers.

Menu

Oui, madame! Offer fresh bread in loaves and round rolls, along with wonderful cheeses, thin slices of salami, olives, salads, and a fabulous cake topped with an Eiffel tower or a message written *en Français*.

Drinks

A fine red or white wine is perfect for this party (for a variety of wonderful French vintages, see www.wine spectator.com).

Games

Guests name phrases or items with the words "France" or "French" in them, such as French bread, French dressing, French fries, and Viva la France. Or, print up flashcards with the French words for items in the room, and have teams of players try to match the items with their French translations. For instance, *fromage* is cheese, *poisson* is fish, *fenetre* is window, *la belle fille* is a pretty girl (attach this one to the bride, of course!), and so on.

Favors
Eiffel Tower goodies (key chains, magnets, T-shirts, mugs, wine charms, necklaces).

Chocolates.

Bottles of wine.

Perfumes.

A designer-type scarf or pin from a French fashion designer's collection (or a pretty good faux).

A sexy red lipstick (try www.bobbibrown.com).

Pairs of black fishnet stockings (*ooh la la!*).

Baskets of crackers and cheeses to bring the café picnic home to a sweetie.

A Little Something Extra
Rent or borrow outdoor bistro tables and chairs to use for your party's setup. Parisian cafés don't line up family-style tables outside, so these smaller tables and wrought-iron chairs are ideal.

If you can, set up your party outdoors so your café actually overlooks a busy street or waterway. Just ditch the berets, the fake moustaches, and the exaggerated accent if you're going public.

Co-Ed Showers

If the men will join you for the party, you'll need to choose a theme that's fun and exciting for them as well—although they probably would love to observe the lingerie shower! Choose from these selections to suit your mixed crowd:

Mardi Gras

Description

Celebrate on Bourbon Street with a festive New Orleans–style party.

Decor

Copy a Mardi Gras celebration: plenty of feathered masks and bright decorations; strings of beads hung generously on banisters, curtain rods, chairs, and tables; bright rich fabrics in reds and purples on your tables and couches.

Menu

Cajun food of all types: jambalaya, gumbo, shrimp or crab po'boys, muffaletta, duck and sausage étouffée, crawfish, corn bread, red beans, beignets, pralines, and bread pudding with bourbon sauce. (Check out www .foodtv.com to get Emeril Lagasse's best Cajun recipes.)

Decorate your cake with bead-like balls of color that match your theme.

Drinks

Hurricanes and other potent drinks in bright reds and oranges. Check out www.cocktail.com for great Mardi Gras–style drink recipes. Or look in a liquor store for Mardi Gras–themed microbrewery beers.

Games

Use bead necklaces in a variation of "The Clothespin Game" (see chapter 8), having players take a bead necklace from the person who says or does the forbidden thing.

Favors

Small Mardi Gras masks.

Baskets of Cajun food, spice mixes, or beignets.

Gag gift voodoo dolls with pins.

Little stuffed crawfish toys.

Chocolates in Mardi Gras–themed styles (ask your chocolatier for her custom shapes list).

A Little Something Extra

Play Mardi Gras or Zydeco music (especially the *Mardi Gras Parade Music from New Orleans* CD) for background flavor, and encourage guests to keep their shirts on!

A Fine Bottle of Wine

Description
It's all class at a fine wine and cheese party.

Decor
Elegance personified. Book or use a room that has plush, comfy couches, perhaps leather chairs, a fireplace, and a very warm and dignified atmosphere.

Use fine china and crystal.

Decorate with wine-colored flowers, plenty of greenery, and lots of wine-colored candles to fill the room with an upscale ambience as you play soft jazz music or *View of the Vines: Wine Tasting Music.*

Menu
Breads, focaccia, grissini, and a variety of flavored crackers; hard and soft cheeses and cheese spreads such as a caviar cream cheese or salmon spread; brie en brioche; smoked salmon; aged pepperoni.

Make it a dessert party to accompany the wines, and stock a variety of pastries, bananas flambé, mousses, crème brûlée, chocolate-covered strawberries, and truffles.

Drinks
Choose a variety of wines and after-dinner drinks at www.winespectator.com, or go to a gourmet liquor store and have the sommelier choose wonderful selections of cabernets, merlots, sirahs, chablis, and liqueurs for your bar.

Serve a vintage(s) from either the years the bride and groom were born or the year they met.

Games
Tasting games, such as having guests try to name the underlying flavors in each vintage (cherry or blackberry, for instance) or try to identify the types of cheeses.

Pull out a party question-answer book (see the *What If?* series) that encourages players to answer questions such as, "What if you could only bring three things with you on a trip to a Greek island? What would they be?" or "What if you had the chance to go back in time and do one thing differently? What would it be?"

Favors
Wine accessories (charms, stoppers, silver wine bottle openers).

Bottles of wine or mini-bottles of champagne.

◆

Gift books about wines.

◆

Zagat guidebooks to the best restaurants and wine bars.

◆

Baskets of gourmet goodies, cigars, gift certificates to wine shops, Godiva chocolates.

◆

Package the favors in wine-colored boxes or velvet wine bottle bags with tassels—very elegant.

A Little Something Extra
Hold the shower at the cellar party room or terrace of a winery, or at an estate home in an exquisite book-filled library or ornate living room.

◆

Host the party in the upscale presidential suite of a fine hotel or at a bed and breakfast where the guests of honor can spend the night (as their surprise gift!).

Mexican Fiesta

Description
A south-of-the-border celebration.

Decor
Bright and colorful with Mexican flair. Use wide-rimmed sombreros, maracas, and scattered red rose

petals as centerpieces on shawl-covered tables; or use bunches of bright red, orange, and yellow helium balloons.

♥

Tequila shot or margarita glasses can serve as festive favor-holders at each place setting.

♥

Hang signs written in Spanish and make road signs with the names of Mexican cities with arrows pointing the direction and mile totals indicating the distance to that destination.

Menu
Enchiladas or burritos with meat, cheese, or veggie filling and salsa; chicken with mole sauce, tacos with a variety of fillings, chipotle pepper salad, stuffed chilies, guacamole salad, tamales, refried beans, black beans, rice, and Mexican churros in addition to a wonderfully decorated cake.

Drinks
Margaritas (straight up or frozen) or other tequila drinks with Gummi worms dropped into them, or Corona or Dos Equis beers or other Mexican brews and microbrews for variety.

Games
If smacking a piñata around is too juvenile for your crew, then buy or make mini-piñatas for guests to crack open. Each piñata holds a favor or chocolates, and the winner's piñata contains a prize or a gift certificate to dinner at a nearby Mexican restaurant or other establishment.

Favors

Packets of Mexican jumping beans.

Margarita drink mix with a margarita glass.

Jalapeño-flavored gourmet goodies in a basket.

Mini-sombreros filled with candies or chocolates.

A Little Something Extra

Of course, play great Mexican fiesta music, or even hire a guitar player or three-member mariachi band to play for a portion of the shower.

Beach Party

Description

Whether at the beach or poolside in a backyard, the beach party makes the most of summer.

Decor

Beach blankets laid over tables or on the ground, bright sunny beach umbrellas over tables or stuck into the lawn, a lifeguard stand, and a set-up volleyball net.

For centerpieces, use brightly colored sand buckets and shovels, filled with sand, shells, and starfish. Or use goldfish bowls filled with water and real goldfish (or, especially if it will be a hot day, replace the real goldfish with wind-up plastic tropical fish toys for guests to play with).

Set up a kiddie sandbox near the party zone for guests'
amusement.

Menu
Either barbecue the basics or go with a seafood theme,
such as grilled shrimp and veggie kebobs, hardshelled
crabs and lobster tails for guests to crack open and eat,
fruit salad, and alcohol-spiked watermelon chunks
served in a hollowed-out watermelon half.

Drinks
Piña coladas or frozen daiquiris; light summertime
brew beers or microbeers; Jell-O shots with whipped
cream (just like at Spring break); spiked or plain fruit
juices; nonalcoholic fruit smoothies; or ice water or
seltzer with slices of lime, lemon, and orange.

Try some of the beach-y drinks—Tropical Pineapple
Paradise, Island Ecstasy, and others—at www.cocktail
.com. Top each with drink umbrellas or the cute beach-
themed swizzle sticks from Pier 1 (www.pier1.com).

Games
Volleyball, sandcastle-building contest, scavenger hunt
(prepare and hide items ahead of time and print search
lists on index cards with summertime stickers on them)
or have guests search for a well-hidden plastic lobster.

In a kiddie pool or across a full-sized swimming pool,
have guests race wind-up or remote-control toy fish or
boats.

Have a sand search in each bucket centerpiece; guests use an extra plastic fork to sift through the top layers of sand in their buckets and those who find a fake gemstone ring (or plastic crab/seahorse/oyster shell) win a prize. Even better, if you use the fake oyster shell, put a fake pearl in one of them for the *big* prize (movie tickets or basket of beach-themed movies or DVDs).

Favors

Starfish-printed gifts: candles and candleholders, necklaces for the ladies, picture frames, and note cards.

Sunglasses.

Beach bags.

Insulated beer or soda can holders in decorative designs.

Inflatable beach toys.

Beach flip flops.

Packets of saltwater taffy.

Gift or recipe books of beach party foods or drinks, such as *The Best 50 Margaritas* by Dona Meilach, at under $7 (check www .amazon.com or www.bn.com).

A Little Something Extra

Be sure you tell guests to bring their bathing suits and a wrap or cover-up.

Set out citronella candles if the party will continue past sundown.

Set out citronella candles if the party will continue past sundown.

If you'll be on the beach at night, get a permit to make a big bonfire if it is allowed in that beach area, and then sit around and talk by the fire.

During the party, play the CDs *Steel Drum Island Collection Volumes 1–6* (www.amazon.com).

Renaissance

Description

Return to the days of knights and their fair maidens at a Renaissance bridal shower. Ask guests to wear period costumes (rented or home-designed) for an authentic medieval gathering.

Decor

Create a castle environment from scratch or hold this party as others have done in the brick-walled party room at a winery or in an outdoor garden.

Hang up royal family crests and swords (make the crests and get swords from a party supply store), and hang baskets of flowers from the trees or wall sconces.

Set tables with silver plates and goblets, rustic pitchers for drinks, plenty of candles that have been pre-burned and thus melted and turned at the edges to give them an older look.

Print menu cards and seating cards on yellowed paper or scrolls, using Olde English writing.

Set a single rose at each lady's place setting, and create the "royal box" by setting aside thrones and a well-set table for the guests of honor. The rest of the guests sit at long communal tables (otherwise known as picnic tables and benches).

Menu

Barbecued chicken legs to be eaten with the hands, cuts of beef, hearty baked potatoes and steamed vegetables, salads, and appetizers. Bake chicken tenders and tell guests with a wink that it's pheasant or rabbit freshly trapped by the commoners, and of course end with a beautiful, flower-strewn cake.

Drinks

Red wine, beer served in pitchers (with or without cleavage-bearing wenches to pour the drinks), and hot toddies (see www.cocktail.com for ideas).

Games

Have the men act out duels for the hands and honor of their fair maidens, but spare them the sword fights and jousting. Your knights can engage in arm wrestling while the ladies wave their handkerchiefs and swoon.

◆

Make up another game for the men, such as using kids' toy archery sets to hit the bull's-eye on a tree. The one who makes the worst shot has to put on the jester hat and jingle shoes for the rest of the party.

Favors
Silver frames.

◆

Single flowers.

◆

Handkerchiefs.

◆

Liqueur-filled chocolates.

◆

Gift books on Renaissance artists' masterpieces.

◆

A fun gift of jelly beans in containers marked as medicine for any number of medieval-type ailments (rickets, the black plague, and so on).

A Little Something Extra
Have a group of the ladies pre-learn an authentic medieval group dance and perform for the guests, bringing

others in to teach them. And, of course, play medieval flute or Renaissance fair music throughout the party.

Best and Bravest

Description
Come as your favorite superhero or modern-day hero. Guests can dress up as Wonder Woman, Spiderman, a New York City firefighter or police officer, or even a made-up superhero (see the Games portion on page 246 in this section for some idea starters). Some say getting married takes courage, and *staying* married takes superhuman courage and integrity, so salute the hero in all of you with this fun, dress-up party.

Decor
Mix the themes of well-known superheroes; for instance, put a web in the corner for Spiderman, a gold lasso display for Wonder Woman, a sealed box with a sign reading "Do not open! Kryptonite inside!"

❤

Hang superhero posters on the walls or buffet table (see www.all-posters.com).

Menu
Standard party fare with added superhero accents, such as Superman logo toothpicks, available at party stores.

❤

Make green Jell-O and call it kryptonite (since we all have to overcome our weaknesses!).

❤

Stick superhero action figures all over the cake, with some climbing the tiers; pipe a frosting web on Spider-man's section.

Drinks

The usuals, but name them after superheroes. Don't forget to drink a group toast to today's modern super-heroes: police officers, firefighters, members of the military, EMTs, K9 dogs, astronauts, or any heroic pro-fessionals you admire.

Games

For a twist on charades or Pictionary, write on secret index cards the made-up names of fictional super-heroes and have players try to act them out or sketch them for the other team to guess. Some ideas:

For Men:

Power Tool Man.

Bench Press Man.

The Remote Controller.

Eternal Frat Boy Man.

Super Fashion Designer Man.

Buffalo Wing Man.

Motorcycle Man.

For Women:

Super Mom.

Too Much Caffeine Woman.

Super PMS Woman.

The Shoe Maven.

The Crafty Glue Gun Woman.

Super Babysitter Woman.

Favors

Superhero-printed toys and gizmos:

> Key chains.
>
> Yo-yos.
>
> Lunch boxes filled with candies.
>
> Temporary tattoos.
>
> T-shirts or sleep shirts.
>
> Boxer shorts.
>
> Gift books.

A Little Something Extra

Play homemade CD music mixes of superhero themes, such as songs from *Spiderman* and *The Greatest American Hero*, plus regular songs that mention heroes (such as Mariah Carey's "Hero").

World Traveler

Description

For the couple who loves to travel, this shower will prepare them well.

Decor

Posters of international cities hung around the room.

Postcards from exotic destinations on each table and the buffet table.

Clocks set to international time zones with the place labeled (for example "London time" or "Tokyo time").

A television and VCR running videos or DVDs of international travel destinations (borrow these tapes from the library or from travel agencies).

Menu
Standard elegant party fare, with a selection of labeled international dishes and treats.

Decorate the cake with two fake passports on top, or with a plastic toy Concorde or airplane.

Drinks
A selection of international wines and beers (see www .winespectator.com), or mixed drinks; international favorites such as Irish or Jamaican coffee, espresso, cappuccino, or international blend coffees from a gourmet coffee shop.

Games
Name the capitals of countries (make it multiple choice to make it easier).

Create a printed checklist on which each guest marks off the countries he or she has visited; the most well-traveled guest wins a worldly prize.

Ask international trivia questions from a gift book or Web site.

Use an instant camera to take "bad passport photos" of guests; have them make a tired or funny face (or wear a faux moustache or dark glasses) and slip each photo into a pre-cut photo holder card.

Favors

Luggage tags.

Travel kits including eye pillows and footie socks.

Travel alarm clocks.

Travel toiletry bags (hang-up bags are ideal for international travelers).

Great pens for writing postcards.

Chocolates in theme shapes such as the Eiffel Tower or a suitcase.

Pampering products for home or travel.

Card decks and gift books with travel themes.

Mini-globes for a desk or end table.

Photo albums or keepsake boxes with a world map design.

A Little Something Extra

Ask guests beforehand to write (on an index card) the details of an exotic, international, or domestic vacation they highly recommend to the globetrotting couple and bring it to the party with their gift. Details to include are restaurant and hotel names, little-known tourist sites, sporting or adventure activities to experience, and must-pack suggestions for the region.

Mob Family

Description

Still haven't decided on a co-ed shower theme your guests will love? *Fuhgeddaboudit!* Just mix *The Godfather* with *The Sopranos* and you have an instant "hit" with a mobster satire shower. The men slick back their hair and wear their best suits and pinky rings while the ladies deck out in gold lame shirts, big hair and nails, and lots of jewelry.

Decor

Create an Italian restaurant motif in your home, either upscale and elegant or with red-and-white checked tablecloths, bottles of wine, and baskets of bread on the tables. Or, book an authentic Italian restaurant for your party.

Menu

Plenty of pasta (see www.foodtv.com for recipes) with seafood or meat sauces, fresh warm bread, mozzarella balls, antipasto platters, chicken parmigiana, meatballs, fried calamari, cake, tiramisu, and Italian pastries such as cannolis.

Drinks
Italian wines and espresso with Sambuca for after-dinner cigar-time.

Games
While many entertainment companies run satirical Mob dinners where someone gets "whacked" and everybody has to figure out whodunit, you might not want to kill off your party guests. Instead, give the guests of honor an enormous wad of play money, and have each guest grab the spotlight at different times throughout the night as they ask the Don (the groom) or his First Lady (the bride) for a humorous specialized favor. For instance, an in-the-spirit guest might ask the groom for a loan to bring his Mama over from the Old Country to get her heart transplant. A heavily bejeweled guest might ask for backing to open her own doggie health spa. The guests of honor get to decide whose requests are worthy, who gets some dough.

◆

Print out famous lines from mobster movies and have guests fill in which movie the line came from (*Good Fellas, The Godfather 1, 2,* or *3, Wise Guys*).

Favors
Chocolate cigars.

◆

Boxed pastries.

◆

Bottles of wine.

◆

Ceramic (cement!) shoes filled with candies or chocolate-covered espresso beans.

◆

A single red rose.

◆

Pinkie rings (get them cheap from teenagers' accessory shops), or even gold chains with script name or initial pendants on them.

A Little Something Extra

Upon arrival, guests receive or make up their own personalized Mob nicknames: Your Uncle Joe becomes Joey the Chin, for instance; and your friend James can be Jimmy Knuckles. Have some fun with it! To make nicknaming easier, go to *The Sopranos* Mob Name Generator at www.rickmelfi.com/sopranos.html to have the site choose nicknames for you when you enter each person's first and last names!

Favorite Movie

Description

Base the shower on the couple's favorite movie. For the sake of example, I'll use *The Wizard of Oz*.

Decor

Set out a strip of yellow carpet for a yellow brick road, and bring in potted trees and oversize brightly colored flowers for the enchanted forest. An artsy friend can create a painted cardboard cutout of the faraway Emerald City to hang on the wall.

♥

For centerpieces, use items reminiscent of the movie, such as a pair of ruby slippers (crafters can cover a cheapo pair of throwaway shoes with red glitter), potted poppies, a crystal ball, or a floral arrangement with Glinda's magic wand poking out.

♥

Linens can be blue gingham like Dorothy's dress, and you can accent with *Wizard of Oz* dolls borrowed from your nieces or kids.

Menu
Standard party fare, with items named after the movie's characters. Make a green Jell-O mold in the shape of the Emerald City or frost the cake with bright green frosting.

Drinks
Cocktails in a rainbow of bright colors, Ruby Red Martini made from ruby red grapefruit, or Jell-O shots in every color of the rainbow (check out www.cocktail.com for ideas on making colored drinks with various liquors, mixers, and juices.)

♥

In party supply stores, you can find drink stirrers or toothpicks topped with different *Wizard of Oz* movie characters, as well as theme-printed napkins, plates, and cups for dessert time.

Games

Ask and answer trivia questions from the movie (*The Wizard of Oz* board game is in toy stores, and other movies have games too), or create a game sheet with obscure lines spoken in the movie. The guests earn points toward winning by correctly identifying the character that said each line.

Favors

Molded chocolates.

Red-wrapped chocolate slippers.

Holiday ornaments.

Magnets and mugs printed with the ruby slippers.

Bubble-makers.

Silver heart lockets.

"There's No Place Like Home" pillows or wall prints.

Certificates bearing the guest's name and award for heart, brains, or courage.

A Little Something Extra

Run *The Wizard of Oz* on a nearby television set with the sound as background for your party, or play the movie's soundtrack.

♥

If someone you know owns a well-behaved Toto-esque dog, why not let the pooch come for this adventure as well?

♥

Check the Web site www.allposters.com for poster-size prints of many classic and favorite movies, including *Casablanca, Gone with the Wind, Breakfast at Tiffany's, My Fair Lady, Top Gun*, and more.

Literary Shower

Description

For the book-loving couple.

Decor

Create an elegant library out of a living or sitting room by displaying a variety of books, perhaps books that will later be offered as shower favors. Use a copier, to enlarge the covers of classic novels and use those for decor, along with famous story props, such as flowers or cigars mentioned in some novels.

If your setting has a fireplace to get roaring, all the better for a cozy literary atmosphere.

Menu
General party fare, or a dessert and champagne party.

Drinks
Wine, champagne, hot toddies, or a variety bar of flavored teas and coffees.

Games
On game sheets or out loud, give the title of a novel and guests have to name the main character(s).

Create a fill-in-the-blank game sheet with lines from famous novels and poetry; guests fill in the missing words.

If you don't want to quiz your guests (after all, not everyone is a big reader!), have your guests pull a selection from a basket of bookmarks; whoever draws the bookmark with a gold star on it wins a prize.

Favors
Copies of a favorite paperback novel or collections of classic poetry.

Bookmarks.

Book-lovers' key chains and T-shirts from www.basbleu.com (a favorite of mine!).

Journals with ornate or feathered pens.

A basket of teas and cookie packets for nighttime reading.

Gift certificates to a local bookstore along with a print-out of recommended books or award-winning titles. Also popular with the literary set: *The New Yorker Book of Literary Cartoons.*

A Little Something Extra

For their gifts, ask guests to give books for the bride and groom's collection. They may be leather-bound classics, coffee-table books, the latest novels, a paperback collection of a stellar author's works, rare or out-of-print books, books personally autographed by the author with a message for the couple, or gift certificates to bookstores so the couple can choose their own favorites.

Sports Theme

Description

For the sports-loving couple and their co-ed crowd, nothing's better than a shower that honors their love of the game. Ask guests to wear the jersey of their favorite team (even with the number of their favorite athlete).

Decor

Consider having this party in a sports bar (so the decorating is already done for you!). For a party at home, hang up team banners and flags, plus all the sports-team paraphernalia you can get your hands on.

For centerpieces, use helmets, cheerleading pom-poms, or containers of chips and dips and pitchers of beer worthy of a tailgate party.

Menu
True tailgate fare, featuring a hot dog bar with selection of chili, cheese, onions, and condiments; nacho platter, jalapeño poppers, chips and dip, sausage sandwiches, meatballs, even pizza. Serve all on team-logo plates.

◆

Top your cake with a pair of his and hers football helmets or a Ken and Barbie wearing team jerseys.

Drinks
Beer, beer, and more beer, plus bright team-color cocktails, soft drinks, and hot chocolate.

Games
Set out a collection of makeup so willing teams of players can paint their faces in true super-fan style. Then, let the crowd vote for the winner.

Favors
Water bottles.

◆

Sports-themed key chains.

◆

Car air fresheners.

◆

Insulated can holders.

◆

Sports-themed T-shirts.

◆

Boxer shorts bearing team logos.

◆

Blankets to use at the stadium.

◆

Look in sporting goods stores for team-theme holiday ornaments, coasters, baseball hats, and even Bobblehead dolls.

◆

Check www.nflshop.com or www.espn.com for team logos, and look through www.starstruck.com for a wide range of sports gift items and favors such as Nascar hats, lanyards and key chains, minor league team shirts and gear, knit caps, and even personalized team jerseys.

A Little Something Extra

If the bride or groom or both were athletes while growing up, surprise them with an edited videotape of clips of their best (and worst) sporting moments throughout their life.

◆

Buy a sports bloopers videotape and watch it with your crowd.

◆

An active option: have everyone go out and play a pickup game of basketball, softball, or touch football after the party. Non-players get to cheer.

Oscar Night

Description

Walk down the red carpet at your own ultra-formal Oscar-night party. Whether or not you hold it on the actual night of the Oscars, this party gives all of your guests (in their finest formal wear) a star turn and a share of the spotlight. No plastic surgery necessary, but jewels are a must!

Decor

A formal dining room, just like you'd see at the Governor's Ball after the big awards show.

Set tables with rich red and gold fabrics and fine china and crystal, with elaborate floral arrangements and candles for centerpieces.

Elegant touches might copy those at the actual post-Oscar dinners: place mini chocolates shaped like Oscars at each place setting, and choose gold-rimmed champagne flutes for toasts.

Of course, you'll need a red carpet entrance. Ask willing volunteers to serve as paparazzi outside your house to snap pictures and make noise when your guests pull into the driveway. Have them use a digital camera so those arrival shots can be quickly printed on glossy photo paper and handed out to guests upon their departure.

Menu

Wolfgang Puck serves over 1,600 guests at the Governor's Ball after the Oscars, and his menu is actually printed each year at the Academy's Web site: www .oscars.org. To copy him, serve Spago-style pizzas (find his brand in the supermarket freezer section), crab or lobster cakes, spanakopita, spring rolls, baby artichoke salad, sesame crusted salmon, and a filet mignon or beef medallions with wine sauce, all expertly presented with creative touches, splashes, sprinkles, and side dishes.

♥

Top the cake with red and gold icing and a faux Oscar.

Drinks
Champagne, champagne cocktails, bright-colored mixed drinks, and martinis.

Games
"Name That Oscar-Winner" has everyone guessing the name of a character who earned an Oscar, and for which role or movie the actor won the award (for example, you name Billy Crystal and everyone guesses which movie he played in that won the award).

♥

Have guests enact memorable Oscar-winning moments such as Halle Berry's acceptance speech or Jack Palance's one-armed pushup (but please, nothing from when David Niven was presenting!).

Favors
Chocolate Oscar statuettes.

♥

Fake award trophies engraved with the person's name and accomplishment ("Best Friend' or "Best Golfer").

♥

Copies of those great goodie bags the celebrities get for presenting. Instead of $30,000 worth of cell phones, PDAs, diamond-studded watches, and pearl earrings, you can stuff your goodie bags with all the same items, only made from chocolate, or toy versions bought at a toy store or dollar store. Include a star-shaped jewelry box or silver key ring for a real gift.

A Little Something Extra

If you have a friend who does a mean Joan Rivers impersonation (or have the budget to *hire* someone), have that woman stand at the start of the red carpet to greet the guests and ask what they're wearing. Guests can be rude to "Joan" or kiss up to her. Have someone capture it all on videotape and play it back at the party!

♥

Interrupt the festivities from time to time to announce the "awards" of the night: "Best Performance During the Trying-on of Bridesmaid Dresses" (given to the maid who dramatically whined and carried on because she hates teal), "Best Performance in a Love Scene" (given to the bride and groom), and "Best Producers" (given to the parents of the bride and groom . . . for producing *them*). Allow the winners to accept their trophies and make their speeches in an unforgettable display.

The Big Roast

Description

Just like celebrity roasts, this tribute party brings together a small band of the bride's and groom's closest companions for a good-natured ribbing and roasting of the guests of honor.

Decor
Anything goes, and no podium is necessary.

Menu
Again, anything goes, but you could personalize the menu by choosing the bride's and groom's favorite foods or meals with a history (a food dish the groom *tried* to cook for the bride on their second date, the lasagna the bride once threatened to throw at the groom's mother).

Drinks
Martinis, cocktails, beer, wine, or champagne. Again, choose a drink that features in the couple's history. One couple advised me to suggest the college drink Mind Erasers, so you can forget those memories from the past!

Games
The entire party is the game. Bring in the bride's and groom's closest companions and even some faraway friends and notable people from their past (a good-natured and still friendly ex-boyfriend or ex-girlfriend, a former instructor or neighbor, the bride's piano teacher). Sometimes their parents can round up some great blasts from the past, so ask for help on this one, and let the roasting begin!

Favors
Standard favors from chapter 11 (photo albums, cigars, or candies to signify all those sweet memories).

A Little Something Extra
Try to surprise the couple with at least one memorable person from their pasts, a childhood friend you found through Classmates.com, perhaps, or a beloved teacher who still works at their old high school (and has plenty of stories to tell).

Deep in the Heart of Texas

Description
It's a down-home Texas party with cowboy hats and boots, line dances, and great barbecued food. Tell guests to come in their country-style clothes; jeans and studded shirts are ideal.

Decor
Use cowboy hats or a clean cowboy boot stuffed with some tall-stemmed flowers and filler as table centerpieces.

Borrow a friend's BB rifle (unloaded and with the safety latch on—triple check this!) to display over a fireplace or leaning against a wall.

Menu
Barbecued meats and ribs, beans, cornbread, and a Texas-shaped cake.

Cut frosted cookies into the shapes of little cows and call them Cow Pies.

Drinks
Beer, cocktails, and drinks given Texas-style names, such as a Cowboy Cooler, Rodeo Red, and Lone Star Lemon Margarita.

Games

Have a roping contest with a length of rope tied lasso-style. Guests try to "rope a steer" (no, don't hog-tie the family dog): a sawhorse, a rocking horse, or even the low branch of a bush or tree.

Have guests write out the names of songs or movies with Texas-style words in their titles, such as "Deep in the Heart of Texas" Or have players make up fake titles for country western song titles ("It's Been Lonely In My Saddle Since My Horse Died") and have guests choose the winners by applause. For more action, have an experienced friend lead the others in authentic country line dances.

Favors

Star-shaped silver trinket boxes.

Star-shaped charm bracelets or necklaces for the ladies.

Baskets of Texan barbecue sauces.

Country music CDs.

Frosted cookies in the shapes of Texas, cowboy hats, or cowboy boots.

A Little Something Extra

A country-style bar or dance club might have a party room for your soirée. If you can land a reservation at such a place, ask if your guests can ride the mechanical bull or just get their pictures taken on it while they act like they're riding. The pictures themselves make great favors as well.

Carnival

Description
Ferris wheels, cotton candy, and face-painting means one thing: The carnival is in town.

Decor
For an outside party, you can actually rent a small Ferris wheel, moonwalk, and other rides from an entertainment carnival company—if you have a nice big budget to do so.

◆

If rides are out, decorate with the other trappings of the carnival. At a rental shop, see if you can get a spin-the-wheel-win-a-prize wheel (or make one, using a large circle of painted wood, hammering nails in around the circumference, and painting numbered sections for the centered spinning arm to point to).

◆

For centerpieces, use "bouquets" of cotton candy on sticks or cones (bought in the store or homemade) surrounded by little stuffed animal "prizes." Set out any toy carousels you can find (I borrowed one from a collector relative), or invest in a music box carousel as a feature item.

◆

Fill the room with lots of balloons in all shapes and colors.

Menu
Hot dogs, hamburgers, sausage sandwiches, pizza (get the thicker Sicilian style in addition to regular pies), funnel cakes (you can buy these in gourmet stores, heat them a bit and sprinkle them with powdered sugar before serving), sprinkled or chocolate-dipped ice cream cones, and a self-serve ice cream sundae bar.

Drinks
Fountain sodas, beer, wine, brightly colored cocktails, fruit smoothies, ice cream sodas.

Games
Spin-the-wheel games of chance, ring toss, target games with water guns or bean bag tosses, face-painting.

Favors
Stuffed animals.

◆

Baskets of toys and gag gifts from the dollar store.

◆

Drink coolers.

◆

Key chains.

◆

Picture frames filled with snapshots from the carnival party.

A Little Something Extra

Hire a fortune teller, magician, or juggler to work for a portion of the party (a special events entertainment company can provide these performers).

Game Show

Description

No Whammies! The game-show shower can be a combination of everybody's favorite television game shows—*Wheel of Fortune, The Dating Game, Jeopardy, Family Feud*, you name it.

Decor

Standard decor, with sections of the room arranged as the "set" for each game show activity you have planned.

For centerpieces, use board games or playing cards from game-show board games (such as boxes of "Jeopardy" questions).

Menu

Standard cocktail party fare (see chapter 6), with game show "eats" such as Rice-a-Roni.

Drinks

Wine, beer, cocktails, and brightly colored drinks.

Games

Play varoius game shows to get your guests in hot competition. "The Dating Game" is a fun one for your single friends. "Family Feud" can pit the bridesmaids against the groomsmen. Toy stores have plenty of home versions of the top game shows of all time, so scout those for your game supplies.

❤

Feel free to personalize the playing questions to depart from those pre-printed surveys and game lists. Just keep each game to 10 minutes or less, to prevent boredom in those who aren't playing.

Favors
Standard game-show consolation prizes—Turtle Wax, Rice-A-Roni, spa pampering packages (make it a gift kit from the Body Shop rather than a trip to a spa resort).

❤

Picture frames for those fun shots you'll send after the party.

A Little Something Extra
Have a fun uncle, father, or friend dress up in a cheesy '70s suit (patterned, pink or orange leisure suit), pouf up his hair, apply a thick layer of facial foundation, and walk around with a microphone as the "host" to lead each game. Center-of-attention types love this job and will make a great master of ceremonies.

Weekend in New England

Description
A New England clambake, actually on the beach or in your backyard during the summer or inside during the fall.

Decor
Use beach decor for the yard, or warm up the place with a fire in an outdoor fireplace or cooking oven.

Provide plenty of tables, groups of chairs, blankets, and a great view.

For the inside party, make it warm and cozy like a New England inn, with a roaring fireplace, comfy couches, displayed antiques, and a welcoming dining room.

Menu

The traditional New England clambake—clams, mussels, lobster tails, stuffed lobster or clams, baked potatoes and vegetables, corn on the cob, baked beans, clam chowder, seafood or green salads, warmed breads and cornbreads, and a traditional cake and desserts (include chunks of maple walnut fudge!).

Drinks

Wines and New England beers and ales, hot toddies and hot chocolates in addition to flavored coffees and teas. And don't forget the spiced cider.

Games

At each place setting, put a "message in a bottle"—a corked glass or plastic bottle with a ribbon-tied scroll inside. Each scroll features a poem or a portion of a treasure map. The guest with the "X marks the spot" for the treasure wins a prize.

Have guests choose an oyster or clam from a pot and open them. The guest who finds your pre-placed pearl wins a prize.

Favors
Lighthouse gifts: statues, mugs, key chains, magnets or little wooden sailboats.

Put together New England breakfast baskets filled with muffins, maple syrup, coffee syrup, tea or coffee packets, and spiced cider mixes.

For cool weather: personalized monogram blankets or quilts.

A Little Something Extra
If you're holding the clambake on the beach, be sure to get a permit for this gathering and ask if you can have an open bonfire to experience a true New England clambake.

Winter Wonderland

Description
A shower filled with sparkling snowflakes and the warm coziness of sitting by the fire after a romp in the snow.

Decor
For that great ski-lodge ambience, have a fire roaring in the fireplace if possible.

Set tables with blue linens and either blue, white, and silver snowflake-printed plates and glasses.

Sprinkle luminescent snowflake glitter or confetti on the tables.

◆

As centerpieces, use snowflake or clear glass ornaments (some swirled with a light blue), white and light-blue candles studded with mini-snowflakes, or silver bowls filled with white Styrofoam balls to represent snowballs.

◆

Hang strings of clear crystals from the ceiling as a light-catching snowfall, and set an old-fashioned sled in the corner for a touch of old-world charm. (Visit www.crate-andbarrel.com and www.pier1.com for their winter-print serving dishes, ornaments, and snowflake-printed glasses.)

◆

Put white flowers on the tables to add to the snowy motif; dot them with light-blue filler flowers. Look for white winter berry branches, paperwhites (a flower), and holly branches to create a great winter feeling.

Menu
Standard party fare, including luscious hot soups such as lobster bisque or a choice of several hearty soups or stews, meat dishes and salads, coconut-crusted shrimp, hot hors d'oeuvres passed or on display.

◆

For dessert, sprinkle a white-frosted sheet cake with snowflake design sprinkles and surround it with Hostess

Sno-Ball cakes, white-chocolate pastries (such as dipped strawberries), cannolis or cookies, and even sticks of clear or light-blue rock candy from the sweetshop. Be sure to have fresh-baked chocolate-chip or cut-and-frosted cookies and brownies for later.

Drinks
Standard wines and cocktails, plus a hot drink menu that includes mocha coffees, mulled rum cider, eggnog, white chocolate lattes, and cookie-flavored coffees or milkshakes.

◆

Check out the ski lodge favorites at www.cocktail.com: Frozen Chocolate Mudslide, Deep Freeze, Broken Ankle, and the Snow Queen are just a few.

Games
Guests write down the names of songs and movies with the words "winter," "snow," or "holiday" in them. The person with the most songs wins.

◆

On printed sheets or out loud as a group, guests have to match the line or phrase to the title of its holiday-themed movie (*Home Alone*, *The Santa Clause*, *Frosty the Snowman*).

◆

Put winter-themed wine charms on several of the glasses to be used at the party; when the music stops, everyone with a snowman charm on their glass gets a prize. Later, everyone with a snowflake charm gets a prize, and so on.

Favors

Hostess Sno-Ball cakes in little wire sleds.

◆

Boxed holiday ornaments (get these on sale after the winter holidays for big savings).

◆

White chocolate truffles or molded candies in winter-theme wrappers.

◆

Satin robes.

◆

Fuzzy slippers.

◆

Boxed strings of snowflake or holiday lights.

◆

Scarves, hats, and gloves.

◆

Blankets.

◆

Magnets with snowflake or winter motifs on them.

◆

Insulated coffee cups.

◆

Winter-print mugs.

◆

Snowflake-shaped charms, necklaces, or bracelets.

◆

Package favors in blue snowflake-printed gift boxes (see www.bayleysboxes.com).

A Little Something Extra
If there's snow on the ground outside, bring your party outdoors for an impromptu snowball fight, sled run down the lawn, or the creation of a snowman and his family—all well-accessorized with carrot noses, button eyes, and scarves, of course.

1950s Night

Description
Grease is the word at this 1950s-era flashback party, with leather-jacketed and slicked-hair studs dancing with bobby-soxers in poodle skirts.

Decor
Imagine you're on the dance committee decorating the school gym. Hang decorations from the ceiling, and pull out those old 45s to attach to the walls or even hang from the ceiling.

♥

Ask a friend to park her classic car in the driveway, and the guests themselves—in their 1950s outfits—will serve as the best part of the decor.

Menu
Classic 1950s diner foods—hot dogs, hamburgers, and sandwiches, French fries with ketchup or brown gravy, and a big sheet cake for dessert.

Drinks
Coca-Cola in the original bottles (add some rum or bourbon to each if you'd like), cherry colas, root beer floats, beer and wine for standards.

Games
Have a dance-off to classic tunes from the 1950s, or have guests finish the rest of a song line or name the artists who performed the song.

❤

Make it a true *Grease* party and have all of your guests name which character in the movie said these lines and more:

"Tell me about it, Stud." (Sandy)

"Elvis, Elvis, let me be . . ." (Rizzo)

"Don't sweat it honey, take one of mine." (Marti)

Favors
Classic-style miniature cars in 1950s designs.

❤

CDs of 1950s party music or the *Grease* soundtrack.

❤

Coca-Cola collectibles from a greeting card store.

❤

Picture frames.

Lightning key chains (a reference to the song "Go Greased Lightning").

A Little Something Extra

Have guests who remember the 1950s teach the dances of the day to the younger set. Be sure to take plenty of pictures of the women in their ponytails and angora sweaters and the men in their jeans and white T-shirts slicking back their hair with combs. Priceless.

The USO Show 1942

Description

Go back even further in time to the World War II era, and make your shower into a USO Show "for the boys." Ask all guests to come in military getups, nurse outfits, or USO entertainer outfits à la Marilyn Monroe and Betty Grable.

Decor

A Veterns of Foreign Wars hall is perfect for this, or you can have it at home. Decorate with American flags and military banners, copies of old WWII posters ("Loose Lips Sink Ships") or blown-up pictures of Bob Hope's classic tours and the Andrews Sisters (all period posters are available online).

Centerpieces can include flowers, candles, or GI Joe action figures and their tanks and trucks.

Use plenty of red, white, and blue streamers around the room.

Menu
Standard party fare served buffet style with "USO girls" spooning out the mashed potatoes and beans with a wink and a smile.

Top the cake with American flags, military insignia flags, a GI Joe action figure, or toy soldiers.

Drinks
Punch, cocktails, beer, and plenty of strong black coffee.

Games
Put on a USO show, complete with a Bob Hope–like emcee, and the bride's friends doing karaoke or lip-synching to the Andrews Sisters, Marilyn Monroe, and Judy Garland.

Every now and then, interrupt the party to announce the news of a "victory overseas" and watch your crowd celebrate.

Favors
Military insignia key chains.

Classic 1940s art postcards or coasters.

1940s prints in frames.

American flag gift items (bumper stickers, car flags, magnetic notepads).

A Little Something Extra
Rent an oversize white sailor's outfit and a nurse's outfit so that couples who wish to can enact that famous "sailor bending the nurse backwards for a kiss" shot. Take a picture of the couple to send to them later.

Be sure to play 1940s-era music; my favorite is *Stagedoor Canteen*, a two-CD collection of true classics that all of your guests will recognize.

Casino Night

Description
Get lucky at this Las Vegas–inspired bridal shower.

Decor
Deck out your party room in Vegas style with neon lights, plastic palm trees, and gaming tables you can either rent or create by draping green fabric over plain tables.

Set up game wheels and roulette tables around the room (again, rent them, or buy play versions in the toy store), along with tables for poker, roulette, blackjack, and even a pull-handle slot machine.

Replace curtains with either red velvet or big gold glittery window treatments.

Menu
Standard buffet fare (see chapter 6 for ideas), keeping in tune with the idea of the all-you-can-eat casino buffet.

Drinks
Brightly colored cocktails, wine, champagne cocktails, beer—all with Vegas-inspired names.

Games
The games go on throughout the party, with guests gambling with poker chips, not cash. At the end of the party, chips are traded in for prizes at different value levels: gift certificates for brunch, music CDs, bottles of port or brandy, and a fine bottle of champagne for the highest roller.

Favors
Horseshoe charm necklaces, bracelets, or cuff links.

◆

Silver flasks.

◆

Candles and votive holders with lucky icons on them.

◆

Gold-coin chocolates.

◆

Fuzzy dice for car mirrors.

A Little Something Extra

Have guests bring a little something to give the couple for luck in their future, in addition to their gift for the couple. It might be a horseshoe, a rabbit's foot, a lucky Pez dispenser, a four-leaf clover, or a Buddhist luck charm.

A Trip to the Orient

Description

Visit the exotic Far East for an evening. A willing host can put on a red silk kimono, a black wig, and Geisha makeup if she wishes, and a male volunteer can sport a kimono and samurai sword.

Decor

Hang Chinese lanterns around the room, decorate in rich reds (for luck), and bring in an aquarium or fish bowls with brightly colored fish swimming in them (also signs of good luck). Hang gold tassels from the ends of red curtains.

♥

For centerpieces, use elaborate Oriental-type floral arrangements (cherry blossoms in Oriental-pattern porcelain vases), candles in red and gold, or trays of sushi kept cold on a bed of ice with soy and wasabi dipping sauces on the side.

♥

You might consider setting the centers of your table with glass bowls of floating water lilies, lotus, peonies, or orchids.

♥

Sprigs of straight or curly bamboo in clear glass vases can serve as floral arrangements or accent other arrangements. (Note: bamboo shoots, especially the curly ones, are expensive.)

♥

At each place setting, put pearlized chopsticks that the guests can take home.

Menu
A range of Asian fare—sushi, steamed dumplings, pork and noodle dishes and soups, gyoza, dim sum, coconut chicken and shrimp, and fried tofu.

♥

Set out packets of rice crackers found at an Asian supermarket.

♥

Pineapple cubes and pineapple sorbet, along with cake, can serve as dessert.

Drinks
Wine, beer, exotic mixed cocktails, Japanese beers, and plum wines (available at gourmet liquor stores).

♥

After dinner, warm up some sake for a drink with a kick. Explore some unique sake-based mixed drinks at www.cocktail.com.

♥

Check for the popular imported-from-Japan heart-shaped tea cubes found at www.beau-coup.com. Just drop these compressed tea blocks into hot water, and it's instant tea time.

Games
All guests holding a certain color of chopsticks win a prize.

Guests open Chinese take-out food cartons to reveal either a toy or a dragon statuette. All dragon-holders win a prize.

Favors
Edible or silver fortune cookies.

Pearlized chopsticks.

Bottles of sake.

Dragon luck statues.

Cherry blossom blooms in glass or crystal vases.

Candles and holders.

My favorite elegant Oriental theme favors are at www
.beau-coup.com. Package favors in Chinese take-out
boxes, also at www.beau-coup.com and at www.bayleys
boxes.com.

A Little Something Extra

For ambience, play beautiful, lilting Oriental music in
the background.

Shower hosts with a big budget might hire a true Japanese hibachi chef to perform at a cooking station, chop-
ping at the speed of light and flipping food items into
the air with great artistry.

Kentucky Derby

Description

Put on your hats and Sunday best for this tradition-
filled celebration of the Kentucky Derby.

Decor

Make it an elegant outdoor garden party on a terrace, or
indoors in a flower-filled room.

For centerpieces, use floral arrangements with plenty of
Kentucky-favored tulips and roses in bright colors.

Set horseshoes everywhere, just like at Louisville's top
parties. Put small mint julep cups (from www.beau-
coup.com) at each place setting.

Buy race-day programs from a real racetrack or create your own on the computer. Have a TV ready to show the race (see Games below).

Menu

Appetizers, finger and tea sandwiches, and a full buffet of luncheon specials (see chapter 6 for ideas).

Decorate your cake with fresh flowers for an elegant, high-class look, and for other dessert items, include bourbon balls and bourbon-soaked teacakes and derby pie (see www.foodtv.com or www.cocktail.com for recipes).

Drinks

Traditional Kentucky Derby–style mint juleps (check www.cocktail.com for the recipe and its variations), grasshoppers, wines and champagne, and mint-flavored coffee or lattes and cappuccino. Or try the Mint Julep Martini, the new hot mixed drink among the race crowd.

Games

If you can't hold the party on the actual day of the Kentucky Derby and watch the big event live, then tape the races from any televised night at the horse track, and have guests bet play-money wagers on the horses they like. (Note: eliminate the strategy and only list the horses' names, not their handicaps and latest finishes.) The winner gets a bouquet of red roses to keep or present to the bride and groom.

Since everyone will wear hats (it's just tradition at the Derby), why not have guests vote for the best hat design?

Favors
Mint julep cup sets.

Silver frames.

Candles and holders.

Silver personalized money clips.

Cigars.

Horse-themed gifts (printed mugs, note cards, magnets, coasters).

A Little Something Extra
Get a tape recording of the famous pre-race bugle call. Whenever that song sounds throughout the event, everyone has to drink a toast to the bride and groom.

James Bond/Spy Shower

Description
Everyone's a secret agent. Ask guests to come dressed in their spy outfits—tuxedoes or smart suits for the men, siren outfits or smart suits for the ladies. And then get ready for a night of intrigue.

Decor
It must be classy and elegant, with fine linens and china for the tables, elaborate floral centerpieces and candles.

◆

At each place setting, put a wax-sealed envelope, stamped with "Top Secret" and containing their "mission" for the night or other game-oriented information.

Menu
Elegant party fare in sit-down style, buffet, or passed hors d'oeuvres. Include International Spy favorites such as caviar-topped endive or celery, fine cheeses, and chocolate-dipped and undipped berries in addition to cake and bourbon balls for dessert.

Drinks
Martinis—shaken, not stirred—Cosmopolitans, and other bright martinis for the ladies; champagne in crystal flutes with raspberries or strawberries dropped into the glasses.

Games
Ask guests to bring their cell phones and give you their cell phone numbers. Using the information in their Top-Secret envelopes, and getting secret-tip phone calls from the party's hosts and conspirators, four teams of guests will perform espionage and spy tactics to figure out who at the party is the Double Agent. Encourage all to use the spy props that you provide: ear pieces (devices spies put in their ear to listen), handcuffs, supposedly poisonous lipstick, truth serum (a shot of whiskey or vodka), even a bowler hat to fling at the enemy (but without the razor edge). Guests will create their own dramas throughout the night and when the Double Agent's identity is revealed among the other suspects and planted bad guys.

Favors
Mini-bottles of cognac and fine chocolates.

◆

Silver cufflinks and bracelets.

◆

Money clips.

◆

Cell phone or PDA holders.

◆

Leather address books.

◆

Sunglasses.

◆

Single red roses.

A Little Something Extra

Think of gadgets and characters from spy movies you've seen (such as the white cat in the Bond films, Mini-Me from the Austin Powers movies) and bring them into the day either by borrowing the cat or having the kids dress up as Mini-Me.

 ★   ◆

Be sure to play a copy of *The Best of Bond*, a CD soundtrack featuring all of the most memorable songs from James Bond movies.

Black-and-White Shower

Description

An elegant party with a black-and-white theme.

Decor

Tables are set with black, white, or mixed-pattern table-cloths and coordinating plates and linens. Find or rent white- or black-tipped silverware.

💜

Chair covers can be black or white to make all seating match, and white floral bunches can be attached to chair backs, with matching single white flowers placed at each setting.

💜

For centerpieces, use dramatic white floral arrangements including white winterberry branches, surrounded by white votive candles and sprinkles of white rose or other flower petals on black tablecloths.

💜

Bunches of black and white balloons can accent window arches or the buffet table, and you can accent a doorway with a balloon arch too. Or, if budget allows, have black, white, and silver helium balloons float up to the ceiling, with their matching or silver metallic ribbons hanging down.

💜

Other options for table centerpieces are: chessboard sets (black and white squares) or a mix of black, white, gray, and silver holiday ornaments set in silver bowls.

Menu

Standard elegant menu fare with as many white options as possible: coconut-crusted chicken, white cream sauces, dressings, or soups.

💜

Dessert can be a black-and-white frosted cake or cookies, with white-chocolate-dipped strawberries or blackberries and whipped cream on the side.

Drinks

White Russians, Black Russians, and Kahlua drinks, in addition to standard wines, champagne, and dark beers.

You can find or rent white-frosted glasses and mugs to carry the theme home.

Appropriately color-topped drink stirrers or themed toothpicks may be available at party supply stores or Pier 1.

Games

Print trivia questions about the bride and groom on black or white cards, and let guests choose their questions from each pile, with the white cards containing the easy questions (five points each) and the black cards containing the tougher questions (ten points each).

Have guests write out names of songs, movies, books, characters, or foods with the words "black" and "white" in them.

Favors

All black and white items. Choose from traditional selections (see chapter 11) or give boxes filled with white and dark chocolates, chocolate-covered candies or cookies, frosted cookies, or white and black jelly beans.

Go with functional items such as boxer shorts, printed socks, scarves or handkerchiefs, jewelry, gloves, or wallets.

♥

Select gift books of black-and-white artwork or pictures, framed black-and-white prints, or videos or DVDs of classic black-and-white movies.

♥

All favors can be packaged in gift boxes in various prints of white and black (see www.bayleysboxes.com).

A Little Something Extra

Create a soundtrack of opera or classical music, or follow the black-and-white theme by custom-mixing CDs with songs within the theme: Michael Jackson's "Black or White," Billy Idol's "White Wedding," Bing Crosby's "White Christmas." Now *there's* a diverse music mix!

Resources

Visit the author's Web site (www.sharonnaylor.net) for additional bridal shower ideas, for information on her upcoming books and articles, and to contribute your suggestions for future editions of this book.

Please note that the following information is for your research use only. The author and the publisher do not personally endorse any vendor, service, company, or professional. Note that phone numbers and Web sites change with the advent of new area codes and changes in Web addresses. We apologize if such a change has occurred since the writing of this book.

Invitations

An Invitation to Buy—Nationwide: 708-226-9495, www.invitations4sale.com

Anna Griffin Invitation Design: 800-817-8170, www.annagriffin.com

Botanical PaperWorks: 888-727-3755, www.botanical paperworks.com

Crane and Co.: 800-572-0024, www.crane.com

Evangel Christian Invitations: 800-457-9774, www .evangelwedding.com

Invitations by Dawn: 800-332-3296, www.invitationsby dawn.com

Julie Holcomb Printers: 510-654-6416, www.julie holcombprinters.com

Max and Lucy: www.maxandlucy.com

Now and Forever: 800-451-8616, www.now-and-forever.com

PaperStyle.com (ordering invitations online): 770-667-6100, www.paperstyle.com

Papyrus: 800-886-6700, www.papyrusonline.com

Precious Collection: 800-537-5222, www.preciouscollection.com

Renaissance Writings: 800-246-8483, www.renaissancewritings.com

Rexcraft: 800-635-3898, www.rexcraft.com

Willow Tree Lane: 800-219-9230, www.willowtreelane.com

You're Invited: 877-INVITE-4, www.youreinvited.net

Paper Products

For invitations, envelopes, name tags, stickers, place cards, and so on.

800 Gift Box (gift boxes and bags): www.800giftbox.com

Art Paper, Inc: 866-296-0404, www.artpaper.com

Bayley's Boxes (great printed boxes to hold favors!): 303-582-0796, www.bayleysboxes.com

Hollander's (decorative and artist papers): www.hollanders.com

Invitation Factory (homemade invitation kits): www.InvitationFactory.com

Office Depot: 888-GO-DEPOT, www.officedepot.com

OfficeMax: 800-283-7674, www.officemax.com

Paper Access: 800-727-3701, www.paperaccess.com

Paper Direct: 800-A-PAPERS

Pearlpaint: 800-451-7327, www.pearlpaint.com

Printsville: www.printsville.com

Staples: 800-333-3330, www.staples.com

Tamarind: 866-296-0404, www.artpaper.com

Ultimate Wedding Store: www.ultimatewedding
.com/store

Wedding Tulle (homemade invitation kits):
www.weddingtulle.com

Wedmart.com: 888-802-2229, www.wedmart.com

Wood Gifts (wooden boxes to hold candy, cigar, bottle
favors): 239-566-3625, www.woodgifts.net

Flowers

About.com: www.about.com

Association of Special Cut Flowers: 440-774-2887

Flowersales.com: www.flowersales.com

International Floral Picture Database: www.flower-
web.com

Just Plants Direct: www.justplantsdirect.com

Plant Shop: www.plantshop.com

Rare Plants: www.rareplants.com

Romantic Flowers: www.romanticflowers.com

Craft and Party Supply Stores

101 Party Supplies: www.101partysupplies.com

800 Gift Box: www.800giftbox.com

Bayley's Boxes: www.bayleysboxes.com

Chair Covers and Linens (colored fabric slip-ons):
800-260-1030, www.chaircovers.net

Michaels Crafts: 800-MICHAELS, www.michaels.com

Sensational Crafts: 800-228-2269, www.oriental
trading.com

Treasure Island: 800-648-0109, www.treasureisland
stores.com

Fabric Suppliers

Fabric.com: www.fabric.com

Fabric Depot: 800-392-3376

Fabric Mart: 800-242-3695

Fabric Pro: www.fabricpro.com

Greenberg and Hammer: 800-955-5135

Wedding Web Sites

For great shower ideas and new resources.

The Best Man: www.thebestman.com

Bridal Book: www.thebridalbook.com

Bride's Magazine: www.brides.com

Bridesmaid Aid: www.bridesmaidaid.com

Della Weddings: www.dellaweddings.com

Elegant Bride: www.elegantbride.com

The Knot: www.theknot.com

Martha Stewart Living: www.marthastewart.com

Modern Bride: www.modernbride.com

New Jersey Wedding: www.njwedding.com

Today's Bride: www.todaysbride.com

Town and Country Weddings (upscale): www.tnc
weddings.com

Ultimate Internet Wedding Guide: www.ultimate
wedding.com

Wedding Bells: www.weddingbells.com

Wedding Central: www.weddingcentral.com

The Wedding Channel: www.theweddingchannel.com

The Wedding Helpers: www.weddinghelpers.com

Wedding World: www.weddingworld.com

Favors and Gifts

AromaNaturals (candles with clean-burning wicks): 800-462-7662, www.aromanaturals.com

Beverly Clark Collection: 877-862-3933, www.beverlyclark.com

Chandler's Candle Company: 800-463-7143, www.chandlerscandle.com

Colorful Images (printed labels and notepads, T-shirts, gifts): 800-821-7999, www.colorfulimages.com

Do Me a Favor: 877-337-5996, www.elegantfavors.com

Double T Limited: 800-756-6184, www.uniquefavors.com

Exclusively Weddings: 800-759-7666, www.exclusively weddings.com

Favors by Serendipity: 800-320-2664, www.favorsby serendipity.com

Forever and Always Company: 800-404-4025, www.foreverandalways.com

Godiva: 800-9-GODIVA, www.godiva.com

Gratitude: 800-914-4342, www.giftsofgratitude.com

Illuminations: www.illuminations.com

Personal Creations: 800-326-6626, www.personal creations.com

Pier 1: 800-245-4595, www.pier1.com

Seasons: 800-776-9677

Service Merchandise: 866-393-9788, www.service merchandise.com

Shower Me Gifts (check out their cake favor boxes!): 866-314-1070, www.showermegifts.com

Things Remembered: 800-274-7367, www.things remembered.com

Tree and Floral Beginnings (seedlings, bulbs, and candles): 800-499-9580, www.plantamemory.com; in Canada, www.plantamemory.on.ca

Way Out Wax (candles): 888-727-1903, www.wayout
wax.com

Wedding Favorites: 714-505-5799, www.wedding
favorites.com

Wed Things: www.wedthings.com

Wireless: 800-669-9999, www.wireless.com

Specialty Favors, Gifts, and Decor

All Posters: www.allposters.com

Brownie Points (brownies online): www.browniepoints.org

Burdick Chocolates: 800-229-2419, www.burdick
chocolate.com

The Chef's Gallery: www.thechefsgallery.com

Chronicle Decks (includes meditation decks):
800-722-6657, www.chroniclebooks.com

Clean Candles Line (soy-based candles): 800-547-5823,
www.madgabs.com

Crispina (blankets): 800-824-1143, www.crispina.com

Elegant Cheesecakes: 650-728-2248,
www.elegantcheesecakes.com

Favors by Serendipity: 800-320-2664, www.fbys.com

Global Amici: www.globalamici.com

Heart Paper Soul (custom CD covers): www.heartpaper
soul.com

Inara Organic (organic beeswax candles and gifts;
portion or profits go to Mexican artisans):
888-688-7565, www.inaraorganic.com

Mandala Connections (mandalas for New Agers):
800-347-1223, www.mandalaconnections.com

MJG Designs (feng-shui and holistic products):
917-655-4751, www.mjgdesigns.com

NFL Shop: 877-NFL-SHOP, www.nflshop.com (also
check ESPN.com for sporting gifts)

Ooohlala (candles and pampering items): www.ooohlalabath.com

Pier 1: www.pier1.com

Quotable Cards (great quotes on cards or magnets): www.quotablecards.com

Red Envelope: www.redenevelope.com

Swallowtail Farms (live butterfly release): 888-441-4126

Whirled Planet (earth-friendly paper lanterns, decor, and gifts): 888-408-0072, www.whirledplanet.com

Wine Enthusiast: 800-356-8466, www.wineenthusiast .com

Woopdeedoo Designs (personalized temporary tattoos): 800-648-6204, www.woopdeedoodesigns.com

Beauty Products as Favors and Gifts

Anthropologie (bath oils, salts, pampering products): www.sarut.com

Aveda: www.aveda.com

Avon: www.avon.com

Beauty.com: www.beauty.com

Beauty Jungle: www.beautyjungle.com

Bobbi Brown Essentials: www.bobbibrown.com

Body Bistro: www.bodybistro.com

Clinique: www.clinique.com

Drugstore.com: www.drugstore.com

Ecco Bella (hair pampering products): www.eccobella.com

EO Products (great massage oils!): 800-570-3775, www.eoproducts.com

Elizabeth Arden: www.elizabetharden.com

Estée Lauder: www.esteelauder.com

Fresh: www.fresh.com

Heart Paper Soul (soaps): www.heartpapersoul.com

Inara Organic: 888-688-7565, www.inaraorganic.com

Lancôme: www.lancome.com

L'Oreal: www.loreal.com

Mac: www.maccosmetics.com

Max Factor: www.maxfactor.com

Maybelline: www.maybelline.com

Natural Beauty: 800-442-3936, www.naturalbeauty.com

Neutrogena: www.neutrogena.com

Pantene: www.pantene.com

Revlon: www.revlon.com

Sephora: www.sephora.com

Warehouse Stores

For party supplies, catering, cameras, baked items, and more.

BJ's Wholesale: www.bjswholesale.com

Costco: www.costco.com

Sam's Club: www.samsclub.com

Books and Planners

Amazon.com: www.amazon.com

Barnes and Noble: www.bn.com

Cameras

C&G Disposable Cameras: www.cngdisposable camera.com

Fuji: 800-755-3854, www.fujifilm.com

Kodak: 800-242-2424, www.kodak.com

Minolta: www.minolta.com

Nikon: 800-645-6687, www.nikonusa.com

Pentax: www.pentax.com

Polaroid: 800-343-5000, www.polaroid.com

Wedding Party Pack: 800-242-2424

Photo Cards and Supplies

For making photo invitations and photo-printed favors.

Cardstore.com: www.cardstore.com
Chelsea Paper: 888-407-2726, www.chelseapaper.com
Photo Stationery: www.photostationery.com
Sam & Izzy Notes: 303-443-7270, www.samizzy.com
Shutterfly: 510-266-8333, www.shutterfly.com
William Arthur: 800-985-6581, www.williamarthur.com

Cake Supplies

In case you'll be making your own cakes and desserts.

Wilton: 800-794-5866, www.wilton.com

Wine, Champagne, and Drinks

Beverages & More (lincludes nonalcoholic sparkling
    wine): www.bevmo.com
Breckenridge Farm Juices (also provides selection of
    nonalcoholic wines): www.meierswinecellars.com
Cocktails.com: www.cocktails.com
The Food Network: www.foodtv.com
Wine.com: www.wine.com
Wine Searcher: www.winesearcher.com
Wine Spectator: www.winespectator.com

Gourmet Food and Cooking Sites

For menu inspiration, recipes, and theme ideas.

The Chef's Gallery: www.thechefsgallery.com
The Food Network: www.foodtv.com
Global Gourmet: www.globalgourmet.com

Gourmet: www.epicurious.com

Gourmet Spot: www.gourmetspot.com

Recipe Source: www.recipesource.com

Event Planner Associations

In case you feel like hiring a planner to help put together the shower.

Association of Bridal Consultants: 860-355-0464, www.bridalassn.com

Association of Certified Professional Wedding Consultants: 408-528-9000, www.acpwc.com

International Special Event Society: 800-688-4737, www.ises.com

Special Event Industry Associations and Consumer Web Sites

To locate and check out the experts you'll be hiring for the shower.

American Federation of Musicians: 212-869-1330

American Rental Association: 800-334-2177, www.ararental.org

Better Business Bureau: www.bbb.org/bureaus (to find the Better Business Bureau of your state or locale)

National Association of Catering Executives: www.nace.net

Wedding Registries

Bed Bath & Beyond: 800-GO-BEYOND, www.bedbath andbeyond.com

Bloomingdale's: 800-888-2WED,
    www.bloomingdales.com
Bon Ton: 800-9BONTON
Crate & Barrel: 800-967-6696, www.crateandbarrel.com
Dillard's: 800-626-6001, www.dillards.com
Filene's: www.filenesweddings.com
Fortunoff: 800-777-2807, www.fortunoff.com
Gump's: www.gumps.com
Hecht's: www.hechts.com
Home Depot: www.homedepot.com
HoneyLuna (honeymoon registry): 800-809-5862
JC Penney: 800-JCP-GIFT, www.jcpgift.com
Kitchen Etc.: 800-232-4070, www.kitchenetc.com
Kohl's: 800-837-1500
Linens 'n Things: 877-LNT-WEDDING, www.lnt.com
Macy's Wedding Channel: 888-92-BRIDES,
    www.macys.weddingchannel.com
Neiman Marcus: www.neimanmarcus.com
Pier 1 Imports: 800-245-4595, www.pier1.com
Pottery Barn: www.potterybarn.com
Restoration Hardware: www.restorationhardware.com
Sears: www.sears.com
Service Merchandise: 866-393-9788, www.service
    merchandise.com
Sur La Table: 800-243-0852, www.surlatable.com
Target's Club Wedd Gift Registry: 800-888-9333,
    www.target.com
Tiffany: 800-526-0649, www.tiffany.com
Ultimate Online Wedding Mall: www.ultimatewedding
    mall.com
Wedding Channel.com: www.weddingchannel.com
Williams Sonoma: 800-541-2376, www.williams-
    sonoma.com

Index